WOLF TONGUE

Barry MacSweeney: Bibliography

POETRY

The Boy from the Green Cabaret Tells of His Mother
(Hutchinson, 1968; McKay, New York, 1969)
The Last Bud (Blacksuede Boot Press, 1969)
Joint Effort, with Pete Bland (Blacksuede Boot Press, 1970)
Flames on the Beach at Viareggio (Blacksuede Boot Press, 1970)
Our Mutual Scarlet Boulevard (Fulcrum Press, 1971)
12 Poems and a Letter, with Elaine Randell (Curiously Strong, 1971)
Just 22 and I Don't Mind Dyin': The Official Poetical Biography
of Jim Morrison, Rock Idol (Curiously Strong, 1971; Turpin Press, 1973)
Brother Wolf (Turret Press, 1972)
Fools Gold (Blacksuede Boot Press, 1972)
Five Odes (Transgravity Advertiser, 1972)
Dance Steps (Joe Dimaggio Publications, 1972)
Six Odes (Ted Kavanagh Books, 1973)
Fog Eye (Ted Kavanagh Books, 1973)
Black Torch (New London Pride Editions, 1977)
Far Cliff Babylon (Writers' Forum, 1978)
Odes (Trigram Press, 1978)
Blackbird [Book 2 of *Black Torch*] (Pig Press, 1980)
Starry Messenger (Secret Books, 1980)
Colonel B (Colin Simms, 1980)
Ranter (Slow Dancer Press, 1985)
The Tempers of Hazard, with Thomas A. Clark & Chris Torrance
(Paladin Re/Active Anthology No.3, published & destroyed 1993)
Hellhound Memos (Many Press, 1993)
Pearl (Equipage, 1995)
Zero Hero in *etruscan reader III* (etruscan books, 1996; republished 1997)
[with 'Finnbar's Lament' and 'Blackbird']
The Book of Demons [with *Pearl*] (Bloodaxe Books, 1997)
Pearl in the Silver Morning (Poetical Histories no.49, Cambridge, 1999)
Postcards from Hitler (Writers Forum, 1999)
Sweet Advocate (Equipage, 1999)
Wolf Tongue: Selected Poems 1965-2000 (Bloodaxe Books, 2003)
Horses in Boiling Blood: MacSweeney, Apollinaire:
a collaboration, a celebration (Equipage, 2003)
Desire Lines: Unselected Poems, 1966-2000 (Shearsman, 2018)

PROSE

Elegy for January: A Life of Thomas Chatterton, Newcastle University
Literature Lecture (Menard Press, 1970)

POETRY/ARTWORK

Your Father's Plastic Poppy, 12 silkscreen prints with artist Roger Lunn
(Goldsmiths' College, London, 1969)
Ode to Coal, poetry poster (South East Arts, 1978)

Barry MacSweeney

WOLF TONGUE
SELECTED POEMS 1965-2000

BLOODAXE BOOKS

ISBN: 978 1 85224 666 2

First published 2003 by
Bloodaxe Books Ltd,
Eastburn,
South Park,
Hexham,
Northumberland NE46 1BS.

www.bloodaxebooks.com
For further information about Bloodaxe titles
please visit our website or write to
the above address for a catalogue.

Supported by
ARTS COUNCIL
ENGLAND

Cover design: Neil Astley.

This is a digital reprint of the 2003 Bloodaxe edition.

CONTENTS

Early Poems [1965-1973]

12   For Andrei Voznesensky, for her
14   On the Burning Down of the Salvation Army Men's Palace,
       Dogs Bank, Newcastle
15   The Last Bud

20   Just Twenty Two – And I Don't Mind Dying
23   Brother Wolf
33   Homage to John Everett, Marine Painter, 1876-1949

Odes (1971-1978)

36   Flame Ode
36   Wing Ode
37   New Ode
37   Chatterton Ode
38   Jim Morrison Ode
38   Swedenborg Ode
39   Beulah
39   Moon Ode
40   Chatterton Ode
41   Ode Long Kesh
42   Flame Ode
43   Ode
44   Ode to the Unborn
45   Snake Paint Sky
46   Ode Grey Rose
47   Dunce Ode
48   Ode Stem Hair
49   Panther Freckles
50   Ode Peace Fog
51   Disease Ode Carrot Hair
52   Fox Brain Apple Ode
53   Lash Ode
54   Vixen Head / What Small Hands
55   Beak Ode
56   Ode:Resolution
57   Flame Ode
58   Torpedo
59   Ode White Sail
60   Ode Black Spur
61   Mia Farrow
62   Viper Suck Ode
63   Real Ode
66   Blossom Ode:Eltham Palace
67   Dream Graffiti
68   Wolf Tongue

Longer poems [1977-1986]

74 Black Torch Sunrise
78 Far Cliff Babylon
82 Blackbird

88 Colonel B
95 Liz Hard
99 Liz Hard II
101 Jury Vet
132 Wild Knitting

Ranter (1985)

140 Ranter
159 Snipe Drumming
163 Ranter's Reel
170 Flamebearer

179 Finnbar's Lament

Hellhound Memos (1993)

186 [1] 'Sunk in my darkness at daylight'
186 [2] 'Sunk at my crossroads, hellhounds baying'
187 [3] 'Me the multiplex moron, multigenerational'
188 [4] 'The very low odour tough acrylic formula'
188 [8] 'Now that the vast furtherance of widespread publicity'
189 [9] 'God bless you little girl the lean dry hand'
189 [10] 'Trouble on all side today up and down'
190 [11] Linda Manning Is a Whore
190 [13] Shaking Minds with Robespierre
191 [18] Wringing the Shingle
192 [19] 'Vapour rises from the ducts and flues, ashen and feathered'

Pearl (1995/1997)

195 Looking Down From The West Window
196 Sweet Jesus: Pearl's Prayer
197 Pearl's Utter Brilliance
198 Pearl Says
199 No Such Thing
200 Mony Ryal Ray
201 No Buses To Damascus
202 Pearl Suddenly Awake
203 Fever
204 The Shells Her Auburn Hair Did Show
205 Pearl Alone
206 Cavalry At Calvary
207 From The Land Of Tumblestones
208 Dark Was The Night And Cold Was The Ground

209   Pearl And Barry Pick Rosehips For The Good Of The Country
210   Those Sandmartin Tails
211   Woe, Woe, Woe
212   Blizzard: So Much Bad Fortune
213   Lost Pearl
214   Pearl's Poem Of Joy And Treasure
215   Pearl At 4am
216   Pearl's Final Say-So

The Book of Demons (1997)

218   Ode To Beauty Strength And Joy And In Memory Of The Demons
220   Free Pet With Every Cage
222   Buying Christmas Wrapping Paper On January 12
224   We Offer You One Third Off Plenitude
225   Daddy Wants To Murder Me
230   Angel Showing Lead Shot Damage
231   Shreds Of Mercy/The Merest Shame
233   In With The Stasi
235   Pasolini Demon Memo
237   Nil By Mouth: The Tongue Poem
238   Demons In My Pocket
242   The Horror
244   Demons Swarm Upon Our Man And Tell The World He's Lost
246   Hooray Demons Salute The Forever Lost Parliament
      Of Barry And Jacqueline
248   When The Candles Were Lit
249   Pearl Against The Barbed Wire
253   Nothing Are These Times
255   Dead Man's Handle
257   Himself Bright Starre Northern Within
263   Anne Sexton Blues
265   Your Love Is A Swarm And An Unbeguiled Swanne
266   Strap Down In Snowville
269   Sweeno, Sweeno
275   Up a Height And Raining
280   Tom In The Market Square Outside Boots
284   John Bunyan To Johnny Rotten

Uncollected Poems [1983/1997-1998]

292   La Rage
295   Don't Leave Me
301   When The Lights Went Out A Cheer Rose in the Air
304   Sweet Advocate

Postcards from Hitler [1998]

310   The Final Bavarian Hilltop Postcard
310   The Amazing Eagle Has Landed
311   Blitzkrieg Homage
311   Let the Thunder Roll
312   Whatever Madness There Is Is
312   Brown stamps forever

Uncollected Poems [1998-1999]

314   I Looked Down On a Child Today
315   Totem Banking
317   Here We Go

Pearl in the Silver Morning (1999)

320   Cushy Number
321   Bare Feet In Marigolds
322   Daft Patter
323   Pearl In The Silver Morning
325   We Are Not Stones

327   INDEX OF TITLES AND FIRST LINES

NOTE ON THE TEXT

Barry MacSweeney made his selection for this book in May 1999, intending to add some work in progress, so that *Wolf Tongue* could be subtitled *Selected Poems 1965-2000*. Some aspects of the selection were left undecided at the time of his death in 2000.

The arrangement of the poems is his, except for the order of later work, which reflects when those poems were written, as well as his wish to end the book with *Pearl in the Silver Morning* (Poetical Histories no.49, Cambridge, 1999). *The Book of Demons* (Bloodaxe Books, 1997) would have formed a companion volume to *Wolf Tongue*: the whole of that book (including all of *Pearl*) has been added to the selection Barry made from his other work.

The selection covering the period 1965 to 1986 reprints all the work (except 'Fools Gold') included in the ill-fated three-poet volume *The Tempers of Hazard* (Paladin, 1993), withdrawn shortly after "publication" by HarperCollins and immediately pulped when Iain Sinclair's poetry list was axed. The early work includes 'The Last Bud', from *Our Mutual Scarlet Boulevard* (Fulcrum Press, 1971), and Barry also wanted two poems from his first collection, *The Boy from the Green Cabaret Tells of His Mother* (Hutchinson, 1968), to be added to this grouping, 'For Andrei Voznesensky, for her' and 'On the Burning Down of the Salvation Army Men's Palace, Dogs Bank, Newcastle', as well as 'Homage to John Everett, Marine Painter', whose only previous publication was in *Poetry Review* (64/2, Summer 1973), then edited by Eric Mottram. *Finnbar's Lament* is placed later as the 'comet's tail' to *Ranter* (Slow Dancer Press, 1985).

Barry did not intend to include all the poems from *Odes* (Trigram 1978), but left no notes regarding cuts. His only instructions concerned a small number of poems which were definitely to be included, as well as his wish to move 'Just Twenty Two – And I Don't Mind Dying' and 'Far Cliff Babylon' to their new positions in this selection. Several of his friends and past editors were consulted for their opinions as to which poems from *Odes* might be cut, and we have followed the consensus view that the sequence should be made available to readers again in its entirety. The *Six Odes* (1973) selected from *Odes* (1978) for *The Tempers of Hazard* (1993) follow the later published texts.

Barry only wanted 'Black Torch Sunrise' included from *Black Torch* (New London Pride Editions, 1977), followed by 'Far Cliff Babylon' from *Odes*, and then 'Blackbird' (Pig Press, 1980) as 'Book 2 of *Black Torch*'. Five other long pieces from the 'Work' section of *The Tempers of Hazard* complete the selection of longer poems from the period 1977-1986.

Eight to ten (unspecified) poems were to be included from *Hell-hound Memos* (Many Press, 1993). The eleven poems selected here are those he chose to include in several readings.

The six poems selected from *Postcards from Hitler* were all written or finished over two days in March 1998, and later published by Writers Forum in 1999. The earlier poem 'La Rage' appeared in *Slow Dancer* (erroneously as 'Le Rage') in 1983, and was placed before other later uncollected poems. 'Sweet Advocate' was published by Equipage in 1999. 'Totem Banking' was accepted for publication by Salt and will appear in *Vanishing Points* in 2003.

'When The Lights Went Out A Cheer Rose in the Air' was first published with a page missing in *Fragmente*, and then complete in *Fat City* and corrected in *Fragmente*. The text here incorporates some later manuscript alterations and other changes included in a reading Barry recorded in October 1997, when he glossed the title as from a comment made by country musician and onetime State Penitentiary inmate Steve Earle, who 'had a line which says "When the lights go out a cheer rose in the air" in the prisons because when they turned on the power to the electric chair it meant that all of the electricity in the rest of the systems drained and all of the prisoners cheered the soul of the dead man to Valhalla'.

Barry also specified that this selection should not include 'any of the other 150 unpublished poems in mss', nor any of the mostly unpublished 'Mary Bell Sonnets', and 'no translations'. The Barry Mac-Sweeney Archive, generously donated to Newcastle University by his family, includes all the poet's manuscripts of published and unpublished work, together with his personal collection of books including copies of all his publications.

The convention used in this book for dating poems is that round brackets indicate publication and square brackets show when work was written. Italicised dates and other details printed at the end of certain poems are the poet's own annotations. Idiosyncratic spellings, from cavalier to mock medieval, are faithful to Barry MacSweeney's fancies or flourishes.

NEIL ASTLEY

EARLY POEMS

[1965-1973]

For Andrei Voznesensky, for her

I am irregular as poker chips.

Her body is mine,
12-string guitar,
Medieval flute.

        (a Matryoshki doll, I find you,
          peel you like a tangerine)
She glows in ballet
  of the life she leads,

   firebirding me.

Ice on the river
river flows deep,

never seen the icicle eyes
of those three dead

Three bullets,
        three neat death holes
        ladybirds on the brow)

        two duels, a suicide.

Burning cannon of loins
blasts me like eggshell.
Clay fires birds eyes.
Water, stone,
        tungsten wings beat a shadow
over the lives of three dead Russians.

You make up for their loss –
  Russia doesn't know.

You make me forget turbulence,
the North Sea in me,

   touch me with your fingers
   look to me for love

Bored with bad poetry
I'm off to Russia,
drink vodka with poets there.

Ball-points and bayonets
are singular in Moscow!
      – gallop through the Caucasus
              with Lermontov's ghost.
My love mis-understands,

              but her name is sweeter
      than bells of funerals,
              her tongue quicker than
      a beam,
              pelvis moist as moss. lips to blood
I am yours,
more than a swallow to
   the sky, my love,
more than a swallow to
   the clouds.

Tell me you will lie with no other.
In case I should topple,
Like a clown
              do
                 crazy
acrobatics,

Steady my heart with yours

   put away old scenes.

On The Burning Down of the Salvation Army Men's Palace, Dogs Bank, Newcastle

They stood smoking damp and salvaged
cigarettes mourning their lost bundles,
each man tagged OF NO FIXED ABODE.

Mattresses dried in the early sunshine
blankets hung over railings and gravestones
water and ashes floated across the cobbled hill.

A tinker who wouldn't give his name
bemoaned his spanner, scissors and knife-grinder,
which lay under 30 tons of debris.

Water on the steps in the dining-room
but none to make a cup of tea

Tangled pallet frames smoked still,
men lounged around mostly in ill-fitting
borrowed clothes other naked in only
               a blanket or soaked mac.

We looked at the scorched wood and remarked
how much it resembled a burnt body later we
heard it was charred corpse
we remarked how much it resembled burnt-out timber

The Last Bud

(for Vivienne)

Here is my thorn, my hate is a bud.
MICHAEL McCLURE

1

Last night tells me today what went
   before. That cruelty, your nagging
sobs, your body rocking and heaving against
   me, a huge planet pulsating thunderously
in my weak arms, weak with the feeling
   in my belly, knowing I hurt you much.
Grasping at thin things for support, but
   finding nothing but books, devices,
verbal chicanery, & cosmological range,
   which no man can see, but writes about
and cannot feel. What's the use of feeling
   intangible things, like some bad actor,
hamming up, hamming life, meaning nothing,
   valued less than that. Country to me
means nothing. Politics, entry into
   Europe, which I read everyday as my trade,
means little, save that for sustenance,
   means of carrying from Monday to Friday
my flagging body and head.
   All that fails to the acid test. I am no
chemist, nor writer. Once I had a friend
   from my town. Now he is a fraud. Once
he was my golden calf, but now warped by
   that gilt-necked stream, he twists about
the stone, and chokes the living good.

I have a friend who shelters me, and tho
   beyond me in years, he is brother,
father, teacher, child to me, who has
   seen him in different shades, have heard
the tensile grasp of music, which demands
   much, reducing me to sleep, as some careless
rock for leverage. He is my friend, so
   how will he take this, this testament,
established as he is, as I wanted to be,
   to be sufficient in all ways, in that
durable fyre I was after too.
   What pale imitations these people are
about me. What castings on the true self.

15

I cannot answer any call, nor am I valid
if I know it is myself lying to myself.
　　What happens when the legacy you search
for, that supposed grail, wretches in your
　　belly, leaving you weak-kneed and crying
into a lavatory-pan? When the one
　　person you really love is 'being torn
apart' by selfish transparency. Pathos
　　of melancholic distance leaves me dead.

I have only one half of my parenthood.
　　The other isn't dead, but he lingers on
this side of breath with the tenacity
　　of a rat. That breakdown in relations
doesn't even bother me now. I just want
　　to be left to be inhabited by my furn-
iture if needs be. Or the music of an
　　empty room.
And the new reality, the real, is full,
　　kicks you over, tells tales, whistles at
you when you walk, leaves you for someone
　　else, but leaves no sentiment (spelled
sediment), nothing to scrawl on sheets
　　about, to talk about at night, when the
bed and the world wait, cold as each other,
　　when piety cocks its capped head, like an
old owl after little, little mice. It flies
　　from the oak, which used to be a sign of
strength, but now is only a sign of age
　　and decadence. Humanity is pale, and don't
grin at this, so young in conception, only 18
　　years this has come out of, a few thousand
hours; mis-spent and irregular, so even
　　in the writing of it, concrete things became
false on the page, prostituted, wedged
　　onto pedestals. The poets putting one
another on stands, laughing a little,
　　slap a back or two. Break a back or two
then write about THAT. The glass floor
　　moves slowly, like the months of mealy
personage. Down into the pit.

　　I am rejected and leave in haste. Today I
read: 'Love is not Love until Love's vulnerable.'
　　Is this too close to the
heart for the telling? If so, reject it,

and cut yourselves deeply, for I'll be gone,
and am deaf to windborn cries and sobs,
    and there is one I know will sob.

That one lends me virtue, and I live
    thereby; she knows the grammar of the
most important motion, the song in a flame.
    'I came to love I came into my own' and
left behind last year's skin of commerce,
    which is a nice term for poetry and friendship.
For water moves until it's purified, and
    the weak bridegroom strengthens in his bride.
So love is all I know, and that the dead are
    tender. What I need is a puddle's calm,
a unit so small that I can span it in one
    go, in a single drunken lurch, delicate
and strong in intent. And not to fall quarter
    way across and graze my heart on sullen
teeth. My heart is bruised enough. That was
    the final lesson. With a spinning head I
listened to a lecture of anguish, bawling
    out of the wet darkness, but white hot too.
In the whirlpool, sleep takes over, the
    boat bobs like a ball: this is the
lullaby of death. Friends and skeletons
    hold hands in the marriage of evil.
There is no evidence.
    Sterility asks how, and I answer from
the Gates of Dis:

2

Some lie at length and others stand
    in it. This one upon his head, and
that one upright. Another like a bow
    bent face to feet; in life that is,
in purity and love, in masking each
    other from each other's parts; clouding
the dense way (dense already as it is),
    and shades across the eye, clear as sunlight,
feeling for the soft heart, groping for
    the plastic spine, to twist about the
hand, to turn into a bow, to fire the
    arrow of the aim into the void.
Reality too takes care to step aside.

17

Even romance sidesteps into darkness at
their passing. Their soft soles, their
   black cunning, peeling the earth with
knives, unable to peel with their hands,
   implementing the very innocence I have
foregone and given up, and now hold from me.
   Frugal though it was then, starve shall
I now, until habit takes away the larger places,
   and age moves me into smaller, smoother walls.

3

And her who is Israfel takes me to
   pity through pain, searching for
satisfaction, which wasn't for me.
   It is like climbing or dancing:
practice makes perfect. Break a foot
   or crack a bone, so wait until it mends
then carry on. That is the indomitable
   spirit of the backbone of centuries
that held down the dark skin of culture
   in a manicured hand. That smelled of
talcum, that greased the stallion's back,
   and pricked the elephant's flank.
That dubious imperial concern and greed
   for guarding those less fortunate than
the hand holding the whip. That dark
   continent of man has lived very well
since this ball of dust aborted itself
   from the sun's legs. So I carry a
burden no longer. Weary, I laugh at the staunch
   proposal of further action, and cry
behind the bedsheets at the coldness of
   my body. As the lover does, as she,
darkened with care, leaves the lintel for
   the street, and the decay of unloving
and the noise of greed. But that is not why
   I leave. I leave for the weariness of
staying the chase, of spurring my steed
   over fences of wicker and match: crumpling
paper houses, trampling on almond eyed
   children, bloodlusting pregnant mothers.
My horse flounders, ditch water soaks my hair.
   I came, I saw, I leave, leaving my sword to rust
by the dead charger.

4

Ah the last version of forgetfulness
   in the raindrops of dreaming. A king
bids farewell to crowds, palms for his
   feet curl under sunshine, while the
disciple (in any book in any clime), leaves
   to the accompaniment of stones. Pitiful
he trails his body over fields, the true man.
   I question the silent rain for answer,
and leave whichever well constructed house
   we were in, from what thick carpet
I lifted my shoes. Which street will I
   be walking in next time you hear me?
Wherever it is I will be doubled, into
   day and night, crawling into one
for strength, slapping down one for
   glaring into my blue eyes. Now I stand
arm in arm with potency, looking forward,
   past both our feet. So just like growing
tired of a job, or some drab government
   post, I leave you all behind in the
summer sun. Enjoy the warmth, soak in
   the lukewarm sea, wave your naked bodies
about like freedom flags. Ahead of me
   is brilliant darkness, and the king
of night. This is a signed resignation;
   I am finished with your kingdom of light.

1969

Just Twenty Two – And I Don't Mind Dying
(for Elaine)

The Official Poetical Biography of Jim Morrison – Rock Idol

From his secret lair deep in grim South East London, The Scarlet Wolf-Boy
has authorised a re-issue of his famous official biography of Jim Morrison, that
gread dead locus vivendi of The Doors. And here it is. – O nostalgia of the
Sixties and The Dope Era! Ohh leather and velvet, vouchsafe to us another
glashing chance of bliss! Locked doom in the bathroom cabinet. Unfashionable,
mean, and brutish (in the Grandcourt sense) – no slag, just watch the way he
walks: 'Wake up cunt you're living your life in bed' or 'I love you, my friendly
little trout of Lambeth Walk.' I adore anything with trout in it. I worshipped
Morrison; I find MacSweeney irresistible in a smoky bar-room. I lend myself
like a lamb and between The Snake and The Wolf, my fire is lit and I'm burnt
to cinders. I can recommend it.

JOHN JAMES, 6.IV.73

Rock litmus. Titration from Springfield, she
wore no colour besides, unfashionable & mean, held
such chemistry in high frond.
  Nothing else to commend her before she died.

Never mind. O Longchamps by silk blouse run
over, meander after crown trimming. Snail on the
elbow, peach-blue.
  Wake up cunt you're living your life in bed.

Down the sequin, par-boiled in acrylic, trim. What
next? Nets across blood drawn-out, let the wrass shiver.
Ivory Steinway for a Fink, hotel lounge that creeps.
  Notice an air.

Blow and she tinkles. Burn the desk, my new
vampire, blousy and blue. Giraffes invade the hands
a chaque etage. Qui? Smoke your kiss.

Chicano fret-board. There'd be liquid over-
drive. That isn't a bass riff that's a copper
knocking on your foot. Crimplene in a trice, elle
a neige, au bain.
  I love you, my friendly little trout of Lambeth Walk.

What do you think I am, a prostitute? Fabergé missiles
and the bell-boy dies. Trim yourself, slut. So different
from the founder of the Shrapnel Wood and Metal Band.
    Oh trite swanee whistle of Greenwich leave some for the
infernal onion.
    Yes?

    That's not a Miami short that's a policeman's blouse
under Lambeth. The building will blaze. Time in the
Trossachs for a youth yet. Red is the colour of my true
love's
    (A tomato in denims.

    I'm glad she doesn't live here. It would be like
jelly. Forced to make her tinkle. That's love.
    Fast licks as a white Les Paul zooms over the derelict
Gaumont. (Pete Townshend.)
    They played through an old tape-recorder for yonks.

    This is better than Eric Burdon's version. Hatchet
the strip. Turn it over, lose your mind, il a neige
au bain go the hounds. If finesse is crinkly you're a
Dairy Box wrapper, whose heart's crisp.

    Palpitating spitfires were the microphone he
used. One's not happy though: the painter died
before painting you in. Rotten canvas, not a
vote is yours. Short-circuits everywhere.
    20 last week.

    Take this black box, it belonged to my
son. Glower was where we lived, his face was
alien. He was not a navy man.
    A corn of skull for Pan. Also take these
pipes. He was a wretch, they belong to you.

Drift like a lady-in-waiting through the tripe. Open
the sand, if it was late. My pimp's keener, un-
surpassed lacqueurs along the baize.

Deck it, asteroid, ignore the Malaga grape.

Bennie's dreaming. Don't tell anyone, sixty miles
an hour in the root. Let the methedrine affected sloth
fly. Sixty miles an hour, backwards.

Ah pardessus d'Automne, sheep wept before
the ruby. A button of mushrooms, along the
gamboge stair. Tenderly ripped, with a chuck.

Umbrellas too, the innocents loved it, the
dark.

Yes there is. Fumé, en Troy. Cassowary of the
heart, pour grit on these inferior spurs.

Death taught to children who could fire the world
last week.

You ignored this? You are ignorant of life
itself. Corn in the washboard, the polack's yem,
buried in a mouth-organ.

Following, il a neige au bain, toujours.

It's either Keith Richard or Stevie Winwood. Shed
noose de leur rêves. A Grunewald flicker.

Planet.

Written on 25 September 1971,
High Barnet, Hertfordshire.

Brother Wolf

(for Jeremy)

> *...the resting place of the savage denizen of these solitudes with the wolf...*
> SHELLEY

> *...and on his part, the wolf had taught the man what he knew —*
> *to do without a roof, without bread and fire, to prefer hunger*
> *in the woods to slavery in a palace.'*
> VICTOR HUGO

1

the fire-crowned terrain
                    as the sea burns
wind
You can't burn your boats when you live inland
Chatterton
        knowing this
Died
Rosy myth
          bee-like
              we cluster & suck.

2

There is so much *land* in Northumberland. The sea
Taught me to sing
         the river to hold my nose. When
it rains it rains glue.
         Chatterton's eyes were stuck to mountains.
He saw fires where other men saw firewood.
One step ahead in recognising signals.
And leapt into the fire.

3

Chatterton (who was no lemming)
mistook the hill
for a green light.   Go! His final breakfast of pebbles.
The mullet used his body for a staircase

They float enviously around the meniscus on a raft of weeds
snorkels sparkling in the dewy light

4

He stood at the coal-face like Hamlet
and struck a match. Eyeballs
                    melted into his cup.

At the pit-head
local idlers waited for news. There was only
a brief burst of laughter.
Underneath, the mole shook hands with english poetry.

5

The mole knows peace and solitude. He avoids
roads and tries not to surface near a cauldron.
Mole lay by the lad's frayed body
and held his breath.   This is no ordinary parterre calamity
he thought (a blue tree
                  grew from one eyesocket
In a spasm of indiscretion
he told reynard
who can't keep mum.
Mole also knows regret.

6

Or
Shelley's heart which later turned out to be
Liver
& the fish had a whale of a time munching english poetry
It still happens
Throwing snowballs at Sussex from Mont Blanc
Toppling into the copper sulphate sol
Out come the bastard files   a
Renaissance for certain
Before Chatterton arrives and breaks things up
With his meteoric tithe

7

All things (and the sea) with their own life
but won't decide for you
A young poet's life burns
Presses
        (july wind on Hartfell)
taking our hearts (and poetry) higher
as if to be cleaned
& not one fish with an answer.   You can't expect advice

from someone you eat then criticise for having bones
because he wants to keep his body in shape & not spread it around
all over the estuary
(and poetry)
Why Chatterton lived in the hills

8

Chatterton knew
you may not return to the source
when you're
it and
died.
At Sparty Lea the trees don't want Orpheus
to invoke any magic
they dance by themselves.
Up there they
strap two
rams together the
hardest-headed
wins.   Death
on the horns.
The trees dance by themselves.

9

He stood at the coal-face like Hamlet
and struck a match. 'Strange
tenancy for ghosts
of universal disfigurement.' Splintering
his crystal
he married the fire
became his ghost
(with appropriate mists
the arrogant say Parsifal

his final meteoric breakfast of green light

10

out of the doldrums into Hell:
'O save me from her, thou illustrious sage!
For every vein and pulse throughout my frame
She hath made tremble.'
Hardly
a valentine.
She hath (a courtly tone) made

tremble. Ann Hath
-away.
A neurotic birch leaf. A trefoil of.
Gone.

11

splintering his crystal
because he wants to keep his body in shape & not spread it around
all over the estuary
rapidly losing the social advantages
of becoming a human-being. The
parties you're always
never sent for. Death
on the horns of the loudest guest.
A final black laugh. O
mega.

12

Shut in
with ghosts.
Restless amazons
itching for a main course
Death.
Black satin.
O
away trembling
ends.
Speak he
said why
not try.
Shut in
the ghost of a hurt.
One strong unflinching hurt.
The trees dance by themselves
and don't recognise time.

13

The heart and
hands
burn. Quick message
to the brain. Beyond
simple colours and shapes.
O
smart.

The poems
it needs to have
to see.
Ghost
of a hurt. Death
on the horns
of a tree.
Elm.

14

Cutting his head
on the rear-view
mirror.
She's river
offers
too-late snow
for a graze.
Cine-cameras himself
trickling.
O
smart.
The priest
saying 'He'll be waiting
for you on the other shore'
and you're always seasick.
Too late
for abrasions
too.

15

Not
for priests.
Hardly
a valentine.
May
your garment marry
the forest not
knowing if
or where the trees grow. Death
on the trefoil.
No one else's blood and muscle.
Leave it.
Bike home
alone.

16

Where
do you appear
when you go?
Ghosting the
footsteps.   Some
one else's
blood and
muscle.
Hardly
a valentine.
Locked out,
you bike
home
alone.

17

I will have Fame
the Nine will be mine
Walpole slew that fact in
vented a smart from the enclosure
Death on a quill
the Nine will be mine
in the arms of Moloch
land of the black goose

18

Bee-like. The randomness of (his) death
the particular randomness
of.   Towards which blood he ran the soft
floor of his eye   A final showing. Up
there they strap two rams to
gether the.
Walpole slew. No rose. No honey
suckle on the vine. The rain
Hurt
with its own
soft density
falls.
No.

19

High hearts
are wrecked.

They fall on the rocks and the rocks
fall on them.
Wrecked.
What are you doing?
Telling you lies.

20

Salt on his lips.
The moon in his hand which is an idea.
His heart-arrow snaps (curare
in soup) because it is a twig.
A road of bitumen is a road to Hell.
A solitary tree in his youthfulness
swelled inside him like the flesh it was
when his heart broke.
It is not Abyssinia it is only sand.
What wet his lips was not salt-water
but the roar of the sea, breaking.

21

Dismembering your lips isn't the same
as remembering them.
Dis is hell.   Remembering,
a reference to it.
Always the same red road
(the scarlet boulevard which for Chatterton
was a northern route to hell).
It is a leaf which falls in autumn like a poem.
Chatterton looked at Mole and did not hear it fall.
For a moment, the poem was touched with gold.

22

A tincture of infidelity.
A poisoned spring
but Styx and stones did not bruise his body.
Angered at the brown splash on the path,
Walpole was one of them.
Nor the cheesey triumvirate of ghosts.
The stone of the mind was god
and god
the Stone.

The road bends across into & up a fabulous rainbow
of precious stones but it is only a 12/6 pill.
The failed Orpheus straps on a sunbeam
for the Dis-
-honoured sword but it is a pill
and seeing the Stone the poet
Says

23
'The whole of Chatterton's life presents
a fund of useful instruction to young per-
sons of brilliant and lively talents, and
affords a strong dissuasive against that im-
petuosity of expectation, and those delu-
sive hopes of success, founded upon the
consciousness of genius and merit, which
lead them to neglect the ordinary means of
acquiring competence and independence.'

24
With lips he prevailed.
Salt on ours
as if life were grievously wounded.
Rain
        hurt
with its own
density
dies. The sun
too.
Who else   but
Wolf is beyond
reach,   the silly
mole?

25
With lips I have prevailed
and a brain of fire
now there are ashes in my head.
I haven't heard from you in months
because I am afraid of that black sea,

not needing the bathers in its foam.
More than a tincture of infidelity
more than a tight cock gathered in salt-sweat.
Standing in the rain is like reading
an inaccurate biography of you.
An echo of a sea, raging.

26

A song in endless white night.
Aguila.   Lobata.   Bucle.
Taken away,
whore-shipped like an onion, orange, carp.
Its wings, teeth and hair displayed
with a neat carnival touch.

You have flown from me, gorged with my heart
You have howled endlessly refusing to leave me
You have reluctantly shaken gold over my nakednesses.

What is left is not a fountain of golden purity
but chains of lead around its flight of fire. –

27

the exquisite car
comes holds all
who go wanting
to now we may
not go
back none now
wants but
stay and
go not
wanting

28

A heart-arrow (his random one) snaps. Red
behind trees is a familiar
deep mark, so
turn to love.
Oh germ-cloud of tomorrow, Walpole
was one, his

illustriously fabricated ruby forehead glows
off a U2 battery for the holy chair.
Trees shiver with human condition &
the temple is thick with smoke.

29

a dream of others.   these aren't
warts this is a newspaper. has
none of
th'Other death
in.
Nothing random or decided in the grey plants
here.
Bathing under the moon which is an Idea.
You
Swelling inside on the saltnessness of air, Air, in
side him for the youth it is, it was
in your black sea, raging.

30

Inexplicable magnets (to human eyes)
Draw out the
Steel. The bull-
head trout. It draws it, across
country, from your
feeble sinking heart. The
heart sinks, heads
for the stuttering plug
& it's a rare catch!
It's an Ideal which is an idea
like eating your best friend. Chatter-
ton ate himself in one brief *rubidium glow*
& the birds lay down and laughed
as the Great Sky Magnet
drew
him
Up.

1972

Homage to John Everett, Marine Painter, 1876-1949

i walk to the annexe
to dust the marine paintings
of john everett
who is out of fashion
but whose work
i like better than anything else
in the museum

the sky is a dome
of madder and brass
and it is windy and cold

a letter arrives
it is very happy
but the last line is sad
and there is a p.s.
apologising for it

at tea time
the street-lights come on
with an extra-terrestrial glow
it is still cold
and as i ride my motor-bike home
the wind makes my eyes water

in many of everett's pictures
the forefront of the canvas
is filled with the overwhelming prows
of cutters
as if the onlooker
were a man shipwrecked
clinging to flotsam
or just drowning
slowly

the park is dotted with people
three men from the park's department
are cutting down an oak
planted by charles the first's gardener
a party of mongol children
on a charabanc trip
are playing with an orange ball

of the only two portraits
of everett

the first noticeable contrast
is that in the self-portrait
he is in a bright blue smock
with corn-coloured hair
a clay-pipe
and a ragged straw hat
whereas in the painting
by his friend and contemporary

he is depicted as a rather
sinister character
with a lean face
dark brown hair
and pointed beard
with a top hat
and black opera cloak
hunched in a deep armchair
surrounded by shadows

but all of his paintings
are bright
with large areas of stark white sail
bleached by tropical sunlight
and deep red shadows
along the mast hatches and deck
and the sea
painted either very flat
or in seductive blue swells
almost like smoke

the rough tasmanian straits
the limpid bay at montevideo
or just cowes week
with a cluster of startling parasols

many painted directly onto sailcloth

sixteen voyages
over forty years

seventeen hundred oils
the only painter
to watch and portray
the last years of the sailing ship

and it is the seventeenth century dutch
who hang

1973

34

ODES

(1971–1978)

for Elaine

Flame Ode

(for Elaine)

Two hawks and a plover swoop
above as we run the
quiet
band.

Listen. The mountain spring is music
too.

(Clear swell
of
breath in
poems.)

We cluster in
the busy grass &
talk. Rise

up & live!

It is really distinct.

Wing Ode

The feet are white boats. Hands are
unlocked keys of colour & shape. Love
me.   Feel me beside you
and within.
(Boats
in April rain
pools)

I break my chrysalis
& Rise!

Walk as a golden man.

New Ode

Indigo robe her arm is wrapped within. Amber
the hair and eyes of this woman. See
them. There, the seal. Is
broken, open.

Shafts of gold in the pale afternoon.

Plover.
Lamb.

Moon goes like
a woman
through time

Un-
broken.

Chatterton Ode

Time is a jagged mark upon the wrist. See
the child does not weep. Or
has any leaf upon his flaming
side.

He holds
what blood there is in
side an acorne-coppe.

Spiky yellow buds
between
his making fingers.

Bread.
Cyanide.

Jim Morrison Ode

Peristalsis writhes a sudden knot &
hangs himself. His micro-
lunch burns.

The lamb in his horned
Calipers moves
afraid. He

cannot find.　　O riff
of my pulse's purple disk!

Sheen & gloss.

Snakes
in heaven too

Do writhe.

Swedenborg Ode

Influx of new crass mourning. Shrouds
draw off the velvet caress a hand
makes
within yr breast.

Is this a Thought-Robe? (See
her gem of mind is a macrocosm.) This
corresponds to something solid
& Bright. We'll

attach our
selves
there

Yet.

Beulah

She walks up. Stands in the air. It is raining
gently and we are transported by
urgency to stay.

You
are quiet & I am inside
breathing slowly.

ICI herbs
quiver
on the lawn. Come

back. My throat
is
heavy with empty
songs.

Moon Ode

what would life be without Johann Boetticher
    or!
        CLEFS DE LA PHILOSOPHIE SPAGYRIQUE

under the pines
of future death

        & Horbiger, owner
            of the leather circus, shades of Grosz!

hideous and enchanting Thulean neo-paganism
            eternal ice of Peenemunde/

            (Beulah walks
            up

Chatterton Ode

sleek beasts
in your equinoctial dreams.

      the song   the song   the song of
      Thule, progenital
      echo of crass teal,   oh peach-

    tilted animal
            in the heart-park
  to whit
a fried leaf of
  cyanide
         oaken saddle
      of premature breath
    the Nine will be mine

    Land of the black goose.

Ode Long Kesh

     & tie strings together
         as the sky falls
between the knees, fragrant
  lard-mouth. A planet in decision. But
       falls sunless towards
  the best uncle, Flapless Man. Sheets & Arrows
on his bracken ankles, terse cloth
       in his worn digital pie. Last week's
Luddite, Tolpuddle broth of caps, Flapless
     leaks
            & the sky (his odd wife)
      fails to strangle inclinations
        between those sheeny
        thighs. Flapless
     never comes.
Flop goes Flapless & the whole arterial mess
       back by the gas with an
        Irish supper. No doubt
     the last of all marchers
      & out for the year.
  Nouveau Flapless in the garments of rich
hunger, living on potatoes & nitro-glycerine.

Flame Ode

'and the warm weather is holding'

        far back, whisky
     nailed the plate, he
kissed an Ace
       On into
overmuch, pukey niblets
in the shadow of the magic mushroom

children held rooms for grief in the mild autumn

And why won't he come, my mother in the pantry

flames shift
in the sky

working late in a crane
              But, he did not, arrive, he
              left

   & a crime reporter reviewed my poems, the
   last bud

with a quote from mike mcclure

          the lion roared back
      sleek beast

    flames melt
    factory gates

   the blackmailer treads over the instruments

        of the poor shift

people have to eat

Ode

Urals postmaster, this is your
dead child! Ecto-
lunch on the shore, spherical
& gorgeous.
              tattle for
a leaf, butter in your eyes
as you fall.
            a dream
of deltas in whose sunken shore
      his weightless sister
    drives her car
            of charity. au bord de la
pollisonne rouge, he struck
            the platform.

      rainy cheeks of the driver on the
train at Koblenz, Monday
 of the year, a
Swiss descendant dream.

    But
clank   another
        point to
  the maquis, altar
    in the offside, together
    by the feminine
        time.

outside the violent plant.

watching the skater's line
swell.

Ode to the Unborn

her name was Bonney and although she wasn't registered
she bored a hole through his iron idiot heart

> Blinking foam of nefertiti
> singular & coral-inclined, lip
> less & many loved, wheel
> your spikeless machine
> towards the sensitive plant
> in a poem by Percy, away
> from the violent garden:
> Speak to the sepal nations
>
> laid down with fathom
> less bit
> umen to follow
> on into the newly
> taken day

Snake Paint Sky

beaming Anaconda of parthian monumentalism your
votes gloss acidly these white stone derivations
I'm forever in excess to

    when sneeringly literal
          to contours

suds abide
      vapour-crushed
borne lycanthropically
      by slippers
truck-hearted

      confluence
    of equally mad
      sources
     electrically
     bridled

  Tenderly those
crackling head-waters
       fray

    to porky
     mitts
    in blood

the sky & I widen, aching

    for the vulva
     clam.

Ode Grey Rose

death beholder
lynx shoulderblade tundra dart
in cold
brother sleep
all of that
  or not

  death reminder
  obituary cremation refusal placement
ganglia warfare in wood neck lace
  panto Plato revives

      death bewilder
      wild wolf eye
        sudden snake eye
      gut button
                    acid
        suds abide in lycanthropic
      fancy tollbridge Amersham

  death bereaver
logs fortify
        damn is dam
                so Elma
can perpetuate his league of sighs

        death betrayer
        believer
    narcosis famine cat struck
            extensions of the form
          poetry sleep death

Dunce Ode

O pusillanimous orb de la Brillo
fetch pseuds!

Agate
pimps my forest
virgin
cigarette,

spatial confluence
of stars.

Pulp & sunupness
your hay was my trial

in my mad brother's
prole tick-tock.

Indulge such wagons-lit.

Juice cups
inside lipstick,
gamboge blue.

Pollen.

White
cone.

Ode Stem Hair

Crepuscular phantoms energise manhood, soap.
Suds of jazz inebriate the mountain,
manners go. Fat city, lush
tandem for these northern dreams
conveying all there is to know
of bread.
Carbon.

Wolves
rise.
Beasts murmur
in lard.

Frig tits when they
lubricate
the starlet's feathered

twat.

Belly.
Honey.
Bread.

Tough.

Panther Freckles

O pulchritudinous orb de la dish scourer,
bring suds!
Fan abolishment, tense grebelet,
overcooked in horny apple fat, muscadet.

Steaming
mind-jars kill
your
cock
song

Cream the city

Gristle piston
inside bone.

Amps.

Clit.

Ode Peace Fog

Cry and she wanders, through
ladders of fern.

Glandular prussic,
fast mouth, turned
on flesh that
knows no bite
though thousands feasted
on her moons
of fat.

Flame lips.
Suck thighs.

Exit.

Fight your hunger,
eat!

Let her come
in leather,
sheer black.

Disease Ode Carrot Hair

Sample the hardness, trite mania.
Finger all that's there,
pus.

The billows are mighty
in a thrush of spots.

Venery
tart lickings.

You want
you say, mindless.
Locked.

Fall on her.
Delight the crew.

Flushing.
Drambuie.

Steps.

Fox Brain Apple Ode

Spangled balconies abound
with webs of murder in
the vine.
Try the madness, drink
rain
& wine.

This is she.

Untouchable.

Moths flame inside her
crimson yoni,
as if she were a Zodiac
in pink July.

Blaeberries
torn from their
skin.

Her horny towers
stand on steel
& shine.

Menstrual poke
of blood.

Furred fuck.

Vixen.

Lash Ode

I put my walking stick
inside.
Its steel tip runs, towards
her cashmere
breast.

Wax her.
Shame the day.
Blame lizards
for the iguana rain.

Leverets.

Fences
& phones.

Apples ground
in mills
are red
and green.

How much you mean
to others,
more to me. Pods

that glaze
snap open tiny

bulbs who eat
my stem
towards the sky.

Cirrus.

Vixen Head /What Small Hands

This is the dirt, far
language. You
turn the consequence,
nowhere.

Fret love.

Back home to
solitary murder
in the vine.

No hair
on you is always
red
upstairs.

Timber trapped
in trees.

Dance without
moving
an inch.

Kiss me.

Cut grass
& urine.

You are awake.
I love you.

What a mouth.

Beak Ode

Open your black-backed gull.
See her, inside.

Fine bird,
hen.

Pearl
orange barley.

Shrink, wear partial vests
of stitchwort
campion
& lace.

(Filters red
&
blue.)

Cave
rime.

Mottled death,
&
Pan.

Ode:Resolution

Pass the aconite.
Wear monk's hood
  ringed with
    wolf bane.

      French words dominated
      Chaucer's day.
           They ate away
      the oak & rose.

  Strangeling
   Changeling

      Chatterton knew
        his way to a
          northern
              Cup. That kind

  of final act
    is difficult
  to follow. He lay down

    & was Recognised
in romantic oils.

      Watch yr breath.
       It will lie
      to you then lie
        down and stop. Blank

  is the colour
    of his separation
  from language & life.

      Asbestos.

      Cadmium.

Flame Ode

Make your naked phone call moan, listen
to a police radio.

Victorian landscaped gardens
mend his
horny mind.

Quit
now.
Cascade your promises
like unfulfilled
stars.

Tawny planets.
Fiery rings.

Eric Burdon
and Johnny Cash
say so.

Pauline
axe.

Fill what's there
with gelded
heifer-blood.

Tups.
Distinct reflection
mirrored
green
& Mighty.

Walled gravy
is a
marriage mess.

Fantastic stick.

Divorce horizon.

Fuck off
get.

Torpedo

Make your naked pencil mine. Play
gradient hands
across this sexy northern
cattle grid.

Rattle
your hooves
on it.

Alarm bells
drink
the seed.

Lavender torpedo.

Grayling can't
match
yr movement.

Eat
hooks
&
wormy barbs.

To win,
suck
seed.

Ode White Sail

(for John Everett)

Show me the door
I can't ask for more.

Sailors docked
here.
Ropes line the house.

Oak-pin
skulls
survive the
China Sea.

Albion, your
waters fringed
with foam.

Everett picks
cardboard from
his master's
trunk.

He paints directly onto square
scraps of sail.

Nazi
Stukas blow
his aquatints
sky-high.

Stolen masterpiece.

Decks recede.

Sombreros tilt
in horse latitudes,
hands sew
thick thread.

Rum.
Tough biscuits.

Brine.

Ode Black Spur

Spurs of neonised leather
smoke the night,
inside a Mondrian
shirt.

Locust purity.

Claire Bloom's
face
has obviously been
steam ironed
into that melancholy
regard.

(Actresses
are magnets to
the common man –

Silk torpedoes
in a dressing-room)

Vixenated threats
of pus
&
horny graphite marginalia
are the
bangles
she
wears tight.

Char bread.
Trout loaf.

Purple feathers
flex against
the sky of my
side.

Tender grebes
delatinise
the moon.

We
suck imaginary
tides.

Mia Farrow

Her wild oregano
delights
my empty room.

Buy
scarab wings,
phallus opium.

Cropped hair.
Pool eyes.
Bud mouth.

Remembered
bevelled cheeks
of
Iroquois.

Beware of young girls.

Viper Suck Ode

(for Paul)

After copulation
Tyger
turns upon her
sexy mate
claws unsheathed.

Fuck snot
gleams her open
jaw.

Mate lies
down.

You cannot petition
the Lord
with prayer.

That's right
Jim.

But
you
took an early
Bath
when a Shower
wd
have Done.

Real Ode

1

Wedding rings & tears. You are on
the edge of nowhere, next
to a moat.

(We
met for lunch
in secret
Soho
squares.)

We cheated
but not with ourselves.

Tangerine
frock
hugs pleated
folds
to
restless
body
Rim.

Happy then.
Smiled.

'I can't see
to finish this'

Right.

Conifer
&
Carp.

Swan.

Ghastly
sight.

2

Quote what's left of loveliness, bend
separation & divorce
into your struggling moat hair.
Orange
fight.

Lips
bowed skyward
in a
smile.

Not now.

Two
of us
in segments.

Pips.

Bite acidly those secret
garden
figs
&
change that stranger's
glare.

Moat bank saplings
tilt
for the sun

Their roots
push down.

Drought
&
Flood.

It's in the
human blood

Now cry.

3

The struggle
is love.

Parboiled,
we sink in the dread
ful
moat.

It is a mote
in our
Eyes

no surprise.

Skull-
crushing crystals.

Bone-
bending words

promise zero.

You walked
up, good
bye.

Wear your
seatbelt and
fix
that rearlight

soon.

Blossom Ode:Eltham Palace

Chaucer came here
as
Clerk of Works
for
King John.

We
photograph the
stark
remains.

Marriage
is
dusty
excuse.

Kiss
tapestries.

Love
is
a terrible child.

You
walk backwards
up worn steps
from the cloven
palace
door.

False queen
adieu.

History is a lie.

Dream Graffiti

(for John James)

Selected from the gutter realm
of citizens
who work
and find no
peace
in pain.
I am chains.

Barricades emptied the
square
of bossy sparrows.
Liberty's love is an arrow.

Flags
of plexiglass
consume my pores
&
the fighters
who
carry them,
torn from their skin.

Let them in!

Wolf Tongue

a Chatterton ode

(for Simon Thom)

> *Go to: Goe to, you doe ne understonde:*
> *Theie yeave mee Lyffe, and dyd mie Bowkie kepe:*
> *Theie dyd mee feeste, and did emboure me gronde,*
> *To trete hem ylle wulde lette mie Kyndnesse slepe —*

        CHATTERTON: *Goddwyn*

1

bee-like
      we cluster
             & suck
Mie blodde steyned Veste
    I lacke noe Wite
Farquars ghasted Holborn flange
      in draped cartoon
lions suckt my death
    quills in my bonnet
from mie Londe be fed
      which is poetry
under the sea. A gorie anlace
    by her honge, Walpole
selling his shares in the future
     of english poetry, quilted
    drawing room beaneries
       foisted on a magnum
    of almond tasting wine
     Ynne hys streyninge
    fuste, eyes
     like sand, bonemeal carpets
down among his mushroom
    windows, skywards
in a flush of finger blood, his
    single intellect blazed
     Gronfyres, scillye wympled
      gies ytte to
     hys Crowne. Terrain of fires
    in a land of black geese
    & rain.

                strev to ryd
                        mie Londe of Payne
                moths
                        inside his moonstone jacket:
                blood pressure 90/40, clonic
                        twitching pride
                                of lions suckt a death.
                        wrath jockeyed hunger, botte
                        falleynge nombers sable. Swan

                                fever defoliated
                                        brightly feathered
                        Aella. Dorsiflexion
                writhed his feet
                                into the living history
                of language, wythe Lockes
                        of blodde red die. Saracens
drained the Severn
        from his head blood, counter-
        feiting
                jealousy
        in a rising star. Snail, forfeit
                your parsley grange. Panther, your
        jet body is a star – amenge
                        the drybblett ons
                to sheene full bryghte

                the Nine will be mine.

                quenched gronfers rodde
                        & anlace sheene,

                                        fanned
                        upwards
                                northern
                        feet
                                vexynge our coast. Acrostics
                early fumed his mouth blood
                                vixenated raven strokes
                on the slain. coffee shop Campbell
                                Bannerman your frosted
                                boot studs flaked away
                        each diamond in the chalky
                                        neonised headwear
                        of his journey north.

        hard-featured men
                levyn-bronde yr brow
        music pealed along
                cowarde Londonne burn

                poised on twelve columns
        ate the shadow of a language
                cooked with albionic herbs
                as he floated down. Crystal

    children suckt
            life their ankles
    snapped into a wilderness
            of speech. storven ynne theyre
    smethynge gore, no prisoners. Their charisma
            shattered into space
                        when he died.

        2
    I ate brondeous Hotspur's rural *rrr*
            my lips inside an acorne-coppe
    I learned in Florence how to poison flowers
        & sheath this quill in absolute commitment
            to a language going north
                without maps.
                Cartoons abounding
                in their brain blood
                bent my face
                towards an Omega
                of horns
        whose presence was like French
                in the dark.

        An ake inside these marrow pipes
                muffed beakless
                    ossianic
                    fakery
        in boundless collar blood.
            Churned to swivelled
                    spindrift
                in a restless family
                of hunger, I
            gathered consonants
                    & stars
        from the six windows.

Wythe a swotye Cleme
and sheene fulle bryghte
this pageant suffered
dissolution before
its chemistry was known.

Glabrous vegetative hordes
extend their fin
into my other eye.

They cool to blood
the tungsten carpet
of my tongue.

I have shewn the romantics
all my drierie Pryde.

Inside this poem
is
a Beme of daie.

3

whanne from his lyfe-bloode
rodde lemes
were fed,

berten
Neders

flashed across a fen
of sky blood, no man so potent
breathes to vitalise
the language in his day.
My takelle
poured a shag of fire
into a heart
which thinks
& swims.

Or let me taste my horse across vast Northumberland
like a thunderbolt of blood: cyanide from

his mouth no

water flows.

yn the Bowke
nete Alleyn
                    to run is
                limed fire, eat
                    motion
                  with rust.

I eat no Latin bread.

LONGER POEMS

[1977-1986]

Black Torch Sunrise

(for Tom Pickard)

> *Who can live with this Consciousness*
> *and not wake frightened at sunrise?*
> ALLEN GINSBERG

BBC monochrome newsreel flickers
        jerking on small family TV screen –
  Sorbonne students hoy parking meters
           paving stones ripped, military phalanx
lowers grinning plexiglass
bodies' confrontation on sensual Paris boulevards
          tolerated hash in Amsterdam cuts down riot-quota

        'our correspondent says there will be no
        repetition of the 1968 near-revolution
           because students have not gained support
        of the French working-class'

Leftists mount insurrection
          neat covert agents ensure safety
    When does 'made payments'
             become 'offered bribes'?
Will the Labour Party uphold the jailing of pickets?
Of course.

– TUC inner cadres make closed door pacts with the Govt
This allows the £
        some relief on the European market
    Bank of England dwarfs
  up the lending rate
    affording confidence
        to other dwarfs/

Circles broken circumferences ripped
      perimeters buckled
    facts revealed
      must be published
because they are seditious

Dragged by the hair students
        on Daily Telegraph page one
  suitable captions
    of a certain persuasion

'Days lost in strikes are the lowest
      in seven years
  The people of Britain are determined
    to beat inflation'

Whipped legs
           of left-bank women students
                    blur on the shimmered screen
                    625 line consciousness –
           systems of response have woven into them
                 a right to decide on issues
           pertinent to individual consciousness, local energy
                    & mass development

                 – plugs are juice-taps
                    inside skirting boards

                    overalled workers come on shift
                    in Scottish grid complexes –

      'At three minutes past eight you must dream'
                 Sir John Gielgud/
                              Lee J Cobb dead, Sal
                    Mineo dead in Hollywood suburbs
                    alleys exploded liver burst
                       muggers' dark blade

                 elegiacs & glittering heroes
                 sour with mediocre filmwork

      'There is work and there is art. So far all
                 I have done is work – you could say
                 I feel bitter about that'

      Lee J Cobb in manly cowboy snarl
           20 years after *On the Waterfront*
                 & Sinatra paid his debts

      no revolution repetition on the hour
        les flics keep low profiles
              hooligan is an easy word to use in Paris
                 for the gauchistes
                 as is sincerity
        when referring to the obedient athletic policemen

              Bird, bat or strangling reynard
              wheeps in the graveyard
              domestic cats snarl at window-sill
              through leaves & long-grass

How many fantasy robot women
                 of university poets
           have 'coral-branch' limbs
                 breasts 'full of secrets'?

Breasts are for kissing
& for bairns' milk
a lovely touchable part
of both sexes

these poets take to bed
          wind and water – monochrome opposites
of reality's many shades

   – pine matches burn
      in coal
   flare because
                    parts of the wood
           remain worthy of fire, like a poet
                 growing older.

   Winds of southern dawn
      blow vermilion gases
         in my skull.

      Barbiturate environment!
      Marshmallow urbanity!

         Newcastle poets
      aim pearl-inlaid shotguns
      on Allendale & Nenthead fells
         heads down behind
                 desolate lead workings
            where John Martin
               looked in terror on the pitman's lamp

         Bunting translates Catullus
               in Wylam
            old as the century.

Pickard lams battered arts council grant landrover
         into cathedral snowdrifts
            on bitter dale hillspine –

         rural economics are a laugh
            if you don't compensate
               for snow.

   On the hour every hour
   Paris correspondent reiterates
   his dirge – snow dances
               by itself in Northumberland
   & doesn't recognise farmers.

Newcastle helicopters fetch emergency cowcake and hay.

Pondwater wine stinks
    raw meniscus on wrists
Less hair on head of husband
    ageing quicker than clocks tick

You chuckle in sleep
    blissfully away
from aweful consciousness
    for a few hours – I stare at you
    in this dark
    which is like a hurt, afraid
                    for your safety
alone.

I deal in secret financial reports
    confidential manpower utilisation documents
        council Deep-Throats with secrets to tell
I must protect my sources
        to weld Press trivia
    in low-key suburban rags.

        Obvious conflict for a poet
        in this predicament –

            to be worked out
                as it goes
            & as it falls
                to be cleaned.

Foot stretched out sleepy cramp alone
    Cooling coals crack and shift
        in London hearth – Real miners
    ripped that coal – to chuckle
        in your sleep, wife, is better than shaking
            at sunrise / solitary

            chic rocking chair
            slowly hisses
                    to a stop,

        Baroque mandolins
        plucked music
            before the next normal news from Paris.

1977-78

77

Far Cliff Babylon

1

Far cliff Babylon, your natty dread future is a dole card
stamped with asteroids exploding
across the city of my
birth.

Putty children,
crassly aware.

I am 16.
I am a Tory. My

vision of the future represents
no people.

Celeriac priesthood offers up my rifle to the sky.

2

Tear the carbon paper of your soul. Virtue
lacking wit cries on the edge
of minefields.

Agents want me to yield. When
I see the Sex Pistols in my dreams I
roll into the garden of a small
nightmare,
looking for holidays in the
sun.

No fun.

My simple body is
a complicated asteroid,
torn
from her
skin.

My life is the size of a
pin.

I have no people.

They represent me.

When we go my separate ways
the colours are dark.

No more apartheid.

3

Hearts like aubergines
cancelled from the garden.

Bint glove,
suck the rivets from
my cymbal,
smoke
vermilion gas. Feel

the city like a river, its
future not written in
words.

Language is a steady stick.

But people are
colour conscious. Their
heroes are red and their traitors
yellow,
Dan Smith fruit skin.

I have cancelled everything and now I am free to choose.

4

I have died every day since I gave up poetry.
Dangerous condescending humans lapped it up.

They stuck their tongues into the gravy and
licked the plate.

Heroism learns to be a stranger
with odd shoes,
too late to use.

Combine your heart with fantasies
of power.
Copulate with the dynamoes inside this
red shirt.

Armband sex.

Helmets erect their tower.

Men train boys.
Fascist tarts obey.

5

Exaggeration is a gift that strays, towards
the minor forest of her mind.
Pineal furtherance smokes, like
a blues clarinet
in water.

She is my only daughter,
torn from her skin.

I would not let her in. I
discovered my ability as
a father
snapped at the wrist.

I ate my fist.

The doubts are bicycle in the
hospital door.

We sucked the floor.

6

The small belief is arrogant, how sick people
move. Hit my bruised runways,
on a council grant.

We collapse in domestic chaos.
Three minute punch ups are commonplace.

My children can
never pay back the thrashings
bashings & lashings.

I represent no people. Not even
myself.

Small,
crawling piety, you deserve
many bombs
&
guns.

I ate your Christian fish.
It made me sick.

Division is your prayer.

1978

Blackbird

(elegy for William Gordon Calvert)

> *if I was a blackbird*
> *I'd whistle and sing*

1

rude unwelcome guest
luckless wind
at family's four doors
nothing fever   eyes wear
solid fern
narrow compass
abjuring life
treason to my instruments
of you   taken
beamed
invisibled   counterfeit
midnight stealer
quiet roofs   pigeons croop
sponge boots caress
aching sills
stare at rough slot
magnets   on the heart
aery chambers   lift
handsome filings
from dust to a star

solid route   distinct choice
years upright to earth
elements
world streets   erupted fuses
smash at old photographics
rushing memorials
heaving thickly   *iron tough*
& curled
drowning love's boat
Russian heart gondola

same hull punctures
deadly violent reefs
fire & ice   teach
beginnings tough
to believe
London shrubs & buds
neat borders
casual solace
explode in nothingness
no comfort   poison

coal with o'erblowing quench'd
vapour forth   flamed
shut & digested to mucus
in swan's belly
fish of sky
hot masculine flame
driven by sleek leathered
foreign chauffeur   whose
visor snaps & gleams
suck in air   over liquid paths
route marked   unblotted
black grouse feathered lyre
whisper to your soul
Newcastle's kindest
harshest burr
melt & make no noise
hands to miss
bunched on a driving wheel
obliquely track a journey
vowed to this trench

sudden anchorites
dust without & stink within
hearth mate   joyous rise
if so I believed
freedom is a current choice
Hartfell grasses harp & sing

discoverer

meet the cavernous mole

shrewdly converse

when timbers fall

thick peat stampings

swift & pure invasion

driven by glade music

total capture   invisibled

veined in truth   no captive

sun & moon also particles

seduced by gorgeous charts

attend your fresh horizon

servants of such final need

old as this century is

2

polish felspar at Sparty Lea
burr the wind with Tyneside songs
skin mixie rabbit from ferret's jaws
melt & make no noise

bunch your hands & clap my head
invisibled by a thief at night
stolen from sleep you stole from your family
melt & make no noise

ruthless masters did not poison you
you opened doors saluting their children
proud to chauffeur rich men's sons
drugged by work you wouldn't rest
melt & make no noise

dominoes laugh in the sun at night
ash drifts down & coats the dogs
fired upwards in the art of flight
melt & make no noise

lapwing lapwing green or grey
singing the smell of earth
sand mingled with blood of lies
melt & make no noise

no requiem no hymn no journey song
stopping to drink from a broken stream
ghosts of miners on the fell
shadowy poachers armed with snares
melt & make no noise

stern with children who grew up wrong
crossing your path when I crossed the Tyne
independence is a wolf that slays
melt & make no noise

follow your eyes to the source of the Allen
follow your hands inside intricate car engines
follow your speech to a wheel that cracks
follow your body to the ash in my skull
melt & make no noise

suck in fire from four windows
blasted kitchen with flaming breath
bear silence which your leaving makes
melt & make no noise

   3
curlew chatter
crescent beaks
ragged wings swoop
snipe song

       long way from Kent
       to your rough ash slot
       which pours
       fills this skull

schooled in grind
taught with pennies
tall on earth
golden man
not fascist Aryan strength
dangerous claptrap

       Allendale rosehip
       whose fruit blood dries
       lichen is armour
       against these sores

we learned stones flowers fish birds
beasts
streams of fact

beck fells
whose terror
waited for my walk

you spoke
punched
            logs flared
sank
      we disagreed
furious
obstinate poles
iron words
fire words
survival language

tears will not
people will
not conniving
emotions will
not fences &
gates will not
bought flowers
pretty cards will
not
callous disregard
will not
            no buying back
            no second chance
            no guarantee
            no trial period
            no refund
trough gathered
pig faces
falcon glances
magpies
stealing shirts
pawning hair
pasting pride
            I want his braces
            shining sleevebands
            greedy bastards
            how much

remember solid tongue
no fuss mouths shut
tight against
light

leave to discretion
who has it but
the but the
but the
but the
dead

do not paint skies at Sparty Lea
do not bring rain to Martin's Haydon Bridge
ignore sun's invitation at Sipton Shield
stand by the Allen at Dirt Pot waiting for trout

       watch the rats
       kneeling
       spit on priest
       & dud employer
       with his sent wreath
don't take sides
nothing left
nothing's right
you cannot buy
you must realise
you cannot retrieve
remember this
       you can't buy
       no change
       you can't retrieve
       hare in a gin
       you can't release
       snipe in a trap
you can't persuade
his heart any more
with toys

1975-1979

Colonel B

1. Orphan consorts & vipers under glass. Hair
        wrapped in knots, secret purple liquid
in her circus fingers. Good morning day
        is love for you at work.

            Electric
            envelopes.

        We flame upward
        in a dream of flight.

            Gash lips, depot
        Venus sinks, sucks, turns
                her secret
            to scrawl erotica. Blind

            men crawl. White
        sticks click, venom. Walking
    men see too many politics. Commons
            pin-time. Shredding machines
            hot with use. Dogs

    shit on the earth & bark. 2. I love you

my friendly little wayward trout of Lambeth Walk.

        Persephone is a gas that kills.

        Trysted husbandry rots.

        Acid bullion fans each window
            from the poisoned centre, we bend
                    will
            to its taste.

3. *She syttes upon a Rocke,*
   She bends before hys Speere:
   She ryses from the Shocke,
   Wieldynge her owne yn Ayre. Right. season fytte
                self ends touching. Blue bliss banshee
                arrow death. Lette my Loverde fitte
                itself a knot
                    of snakes, scorpion burning
            million sand eyes. Uncouth brute. Stinking yob.

                    Collared neckblood, finger shit,
                duff born bastard, entrance wrong way.
            Mercy is Xtian
no mercy no molotov me. No bash
                    but kiss –
            not foot. Your little games
            secret. Pretty shirt
                    joy
                        shared not. 4. Patchy dark
overtakes the bloody mistress of his pleasant ayre.
        Blood whose with my waters fat flow thick. sonke
            in bloode, neck charts, grim Juga:
                burn pansies, parsley vlix, pick-your-mother's-
eyes–out, purging flax. Rip chicken legs (rhode island sussex)
            out of it. Pisspoor jackdaws bark
                long legged gnawed by filthy cats
                & stinking canine flesh.
                        Butchers
            all I see. Flesh hanging
            off the bone & hooks. Burning
                    books. Taj Mahals
            of muttshit, people
        eating anthrax virus. Horned
            fuckdust plugs their eyes.

INHILDE SOMEJOICE OF LYFE, OR ELSE MY DEARE
                    (LOVE DIES –

            burn yr halles of merriement – burst
            yr miskynettes.

        Sack the scallywag who brought me to this
                fucking awful place.

5.   Elated surgeon, second honeymoon ragged to ribbons
                by freedom Belfast housefrau
                    obsessed with her / nothing has moved /
engages the characters/ stunningly/ mummers
            aiming red guns, lonely passionated
            gum blood, fire, spitting house flame,
                cold bodies in what happens next is
a victorian collection of demesning smut. 6. to find
            out 10 years younger why this happened
                her hair streaked with splendidly bracing
    experience.   Precious few female
                    erotic forces can knot
                such deadly nightshade

Merk Plantes in her
fingers
for so many
lovers to
suck
the poison down.

I to the Qwood muste goe because there is more cash in It.
Arts Councils
I suck dry. Blacklists
stuff my mind. Col B's name
(JOHNSTON) writ large in letters scraped
on Whitley Bay's famous golden shore.
Where waves roar
inside the cardboard heads
of grey overcoats
with writs to serve. We swerve.
7.   Drybblet joie maie find a beme of bacon rind, inshore, when
it he she they come
home (where violence is & was). Yem is where
people die, mindblood
draining into hearths from hearts. Slaver
drips from every pore
you see. It
will cost nothing. You will be refunded
for this so-called truth.
Your house will have kernels of gold
laid upon its roof.
Piss on it & pull
nettle roots from your plan. Gourmets
in evasion spick petal dust up
fucked kind like.
none wife go/sweater pretty shirt/thread politics/explain/apologise
burned relief I come from bulls, creased amoeba
hit the fan of all delights, cataract, blind pastry
ducks, sways, seeks
ENHELE ME/CAST NO SHRED. 8. Come far in years.
Sample hard mania lies.   Sample rubber policies.
Swallow stiff wrists embalmed with sable tongue.
Learn gristle kidda. Learn scumbag frown.
Learn slap on head
or you'll stay in for life.   belted arse, slave tactics.
Plit quote love poems to reach jowhere: 8. meant split love's
mayakovsky boat bolshevik bad translation
GONDOLA on vodka Neva
future/wrist/stick plimsoll geometry
of the hardened spirit

bent back to sky
canvas slashed,
anonymous goths,
heavy european rain (rulers, federalists, kings).

Tsar me.   King me.   Secretariat my joys.   Bureaucratise
loves, hair. Bind this
muscled canopy & cook it dry. Scrape
gravy from heart's disease, curious
disquiet of the soul.
Bondage is a SCORE OF STEDES
to Ride Me from this Arid Plain. Get
whatte I know is nowt, sunny Jims
so filled with valley
rain. HARTE
SYKE PEYNE, middle english sense
I know tonight or any day
of dreams that clash. Fash not
ligamentisity, fresh language, pulsing
velour cravats, fannies
of famous women,
doggie carrots, eyes swivelled
in a mirror of their own reflections. We
learn page one, page three, banner trash.

Queen me! Ha! Princess pearl toes
120-point princess Cinderella, what bedbait. Kiss

then. Bend under rain. **9.** Last buds

come first. Come back. Lions
are their fear. Maned kayaks
in the rough of life. Thorn
roots – I have their
word for it – pull
DOWN.

Snap   Snap   Snap.   Trench is life. Rut is go.

Blending was post-Swedenborgian, cherries **10.**
fell from the cake house. We learned
many. Sheen peeled. Lacquer lost its somehow
in the gale. Too small
a guyfte the londe & sea, you spread
a shield whose argent. Whose argent
burned up sight sound.

I was Aella's slave. I ate words.
I was Aella's wife. No holpe came quick.
I was Aella's labourer. He broke my axe.
I was Aella's lover. We made amends.
I was Aella's universe. We settled for sandgrains.

O save me from her thou illustrious sage
is a herbal telegram whose text (nicked from Dante)
enchained
moi, would not keep us from the flames
of Dis.
Hear this.
Your
secret 11. games
tempt to wrong beds. Drawn by conduits
of red hair
up
sleek
gunbarrels in the rain, gutter
stealth, I
rode gondola's nightshirt waves & sank
a shaft to hilt
in molten sand. Betraste, coptic,
this is the network, ancient brother
in arms, hand
by loin.
I seek your groin
with a stone.

12. CELMONDE is a lover I would skin sheets to seek.
Pleats in her many-furrowed glebe
as she speaks queen's speech

: POTTE OUT POTTE OUT
melt these plastic bicycle
itinerary's dark stream
clash events:
marrows, young rhubarb
stainless bint is number 10
no glove on cattle grid this horn whose hooves
spark furnace night. We eat
red snow. F1 hybrid
St John Stevas grin at Bexley Ted
hair on hair shirt before cameras, Bede's sandals
Cuthbert's
cannot walk this land. His
hut

is cut
by hand
while private practice thrives. Weep in drizzle
of raincoat doubled majorities. THE MAGGIES
BEATS. THE MAGGIE BOEAST.

The Maggie Beast

fire amalgam, mercury poisoning
tubed cadmium, delta mouth
mudlips on stroking maps

Albion, a new geography
Albion, to be repealed.

IAM NO SHIELD.

Open the door.

Rented skies.

Colour bleeds to horizon's rim.

Quest is claw.

(coda)

Betelgeuse. My central star.

Justice as geography of the soul.

Opportunity is darkness. I am

16. I am
a Tory. I am sixteen
different stories.
The moon (Beulah) walks Up.
She is white torch maiden
protected by blue police of the night.
No frights
distress her
glowing
garment hem.
Plexistars,
windows of the mind, cloches
thrown up reflecting
dawn, so blind
each pace towards the door.

Sunken breath,
saucer eyes, no
surprise. Up for sale
we go, driven into
roots
by blood & silence
of our lives.

1978-79
this state of the nation bulletin for J.H. Prynne

Liz Hard

LIZ HARD VERY HARD

Kein Eingang Liz gone hard from the broken phallic window.
   Liz mammoth burning windgrass turned.
     Liz trunk spewing water from the man.
Liz jam. Liz lintblood.
      Liz cracking leg open secret doorpost fool.

  Liz pill moaning. Liz lust. Liz ate salt & came wild.
Liz lipped asterisks cancelling all flame.

  Liz pulling dogrose from the horny cowslip lawn.
    Victorian women chewing couchgrass ate up Liz.

     FizzLiz lay like figs on Jordan.

  Liz burned beads & sank her sandals fast.
  Liz got smoked & crushed up. Liz lolled.

  Tough Liz kicked off her feet & made a stand.

   Bonfire Liz poked punks. Her embers swelled.

    Big Liz came small. Small Liz came Big.

    Ungloved Liz moved fingers like a harpist.

  Liz leapt like a lamb in clover.
    Liz rolled over.
Liz died & smiled her Lazarus way back.

  Wagner hag Liz terrified when sturms blacked up.
Liz lay foxbrush ruffled vixen bloode.

    Venus mounds filled the steamy satin bedroom sheets
Liz did.
    I've got the high heels if you've got the lips
      said honeyheart Liz.
   Liz grinned & hid.
 I don't want to be your mother I want to be your childe
  Astrakhan Liz crowed dawnwild.

 Bathfoam Liz urged suck my tits to watercress.
  Bastard bonehard Liz banned the bloody Press.

 Festering pigpens perked Liz's lather to funfoam.
Liz was Vauxhall Viva fins & Liz was mustard chrome.

Liz lay her whistle on the harbour bunk.
Itch me or I'm sunk
wrote Paris postcard Liz.

Her loins in Boulogne. Her shoes in Toulouse.

La Liz.

Cap Gris Nez Liz.

Gin Fizz Liz.

LIZ SINGS INNOCENCE IS TRUE

Fix yr vengeance.
ANKLE STRAPLETS
TURNED IN GOLD AUX PERLES DE LA JAPON.

Navy lacewing eyeshadow streamer stick
brushed Maltese civil servant lips
gone REALLY PURPLE MIDNIGHT PUNK.

Strobelight disco Liz all funked Up.

CURSED WIRES STRAPPED HER
ANKLES TO THE BED. LIZ MOANED
FREE ME
FROM MAKING FLOWERS
FOR THE SHELF
& HERBAL WIFELIKE HUSBANDRY.

FUSE HER JAVA
GLEAMING
CONCHES'
HORNY AMBER
JADE
TO NAZI BEDCLOTHES
MADE BY MUM.

Split bint. Bang all prism windows.

Porn doors explode!

BREEZY FUCKLARD TITPIG, YOU WON'T
SURVIVE
ANOTHER GLITTERING SWEATSHOP DAYLONG
 HOUR AT THE BLITZKRIEG
            DEADLINE SPEWSHIFT. YOU'LL CLAP
            NEWSDESK HANDS
TOO OFTEN AT MURDER FOR BREAKFAST &
            NIGHTCAP FIRES
      WHEN THE VIXENATED HORN-ON
      DAWN RULES
            BIZARRE SHOES IN SEX DEATH

            OBSOLETE
         AS FARM PRICES
         EVERYWHERE.

   JUNKIE RUSHES PUMPING CORAZON
      DOWN HOTLINE WIRES

  WILL BURN EACH JUNCTION
                LIKE A NAZI BOOK.

I am stopping you Kein Eingang. Cannot speak English.
        Virgin no wives no husbands. Sheer attack
stops mouth lip fiasco. No jewels up me, no gems, no
        stars. Stop you. Stop. This way please.
        My husband is UK. Bring passport.
Luggage will be collected & searched. Strip down.

            BEND OVER NOW.

            Digit Durex

MIDDLE FINGER WIGGLING FOR EMERALDS, HASH
                &

   CHICKEN KORMA BANANA PULP
         WORM-EATEN

         TURDS.

Liz ruts harbour cool: DO IT DOGGIE/DO IT NOW NOW.
No Soviet sowlust here, honked high-tide Liz, smothering
     Johnson's baby swandown talc on plastic
         plexitits & nipple neon.
Let's burn a boozy bed in Honfleur
                 quarrelled hardhat Liz:
                 gleaming
   visors snapped a skyblue halt.
  Liz crapped on Calais campgrass: BACK YR BRASCUM
    ANTLER ROSIN
              INTO THE TARTAN PENCIL HOLDER
         WHERE MY SHINY SHOULDERS
      LEAVE THE GRANULATED WHEEL.

Sturmed Brunhilde Liz: dump your Marks & Sparks safari suit
    in the single sleeping-bag.

    Pull the pin by pushing in.
  Frig the trigger & make it bigger.
   Skim the quim & make it swim.
   Flit the clit.

MAKE IT SLICKER & MAKE IT QUICKER.

Lanzarote Liz firing on all Sealink cylinders stoking up the coke hole
    on duty free lust & gin!!

Liz Hard II

NAZI neon burned the blitzkrieg heart Liz hid.
    Mascara fish-eye stares sank each blondette from the console desk.
Pulping guns prodded every uplift bra.

    Liz longed for the double-fist grip looking down with magnum force.

        Trigger me, I'm hotter than a cartridge, wooed voodoo Liz.
                Let me bead a victim or I can't come.

        Fill my chambers. Pump me redhot. Blast
           each lipstick quimtrick.

        Lovely, lisped Liz, hissing through the air her baton rouge.
                Handcuff jewellery gleamed.
        Snap me tight, I'll swing on your wrist.

        No hanky-panky Beano comic dramas in this cylinder
                of light
                Liz touched up
the steely Peenemunde penis
                    she would rocket
                    if she could.

Zap me, strap me, tie me down. I'll struggle! Spit!
           Venom is the tricky horn in me.
Make my head strange, my armband hands & Stuka divebomb sex.

Bind with silkstraps this fuming lustbulb till high-heeled cows
           come home. Butter me
now & DO IT doggie pigpig, REALLY FAST &
    KNIFESHARP!

        Don't meadow me with glebe lips & a farting lute!
        I haven't got TCHAIKOVSKY TITS OR A DELIUS DANGLING
           TWAT.

Keep yr Poussin pussy pushes for the underarm deodorant queens.

        Talcum me, certainly, but send it down like SNOW-GRIT.

La Liz lectured: Beethoven's a bang,
               but Schubert
               is a thigh-suck,
               mortgaged
               to the hilt
               with brains.

Sperm it, chunkdream, make the chartreuse sweaterdress sticky juice-gum.
  Spastic yr twitch-root, pinkspam truncheon luncheonette.

      KNIT ME NICELY AND I'LL BELT! BUTTON
        YOU UP!
      FONDLE ALL THE ESTEE LAUDER BINT
        TRASH & I'LL SQUEAL!
      Keep their cinnamon eyelid rivers at bay. I'm clean.

  Beribbon all these treacherous gunbarrel babies, & I'll stink
  yr nose with puckered bumjug curds, creamy ever so!

You'll not flail me with missionary scissor vulva sucks, nipple
  postcards so sweet to be here, fucktoes swooning on the latch.

    Let your ferret free to pug & drum. Nip & stoat.

    Rivet, skewer, wheel in the screws.

            Thing it, HARD.

          Groin me with a blade.

May-June 1982

Jury Vet

LOVE IS THE DRUG AND YOU NEED TO SCORE

OKAY CRIMSON VARNISHED REDHEAD YOU'RE
THE BIG ATTRACTION NOW.

gamboge star-crusher, ferrous corazon,
filament kisses, adder
meltings,
no
chance pain.
Tour my body and fetch me Rain.

———————————————

Let me chew all of your Shoes.

———————————————

Thrillbox arias in the lust of tampon grandeur.
Frill tease stockingtop flames.
Sue cancels each Deneuving rivulet of horn.
Swelling lapus cuffchunks,
yoni triggered like a frigidaire
in a
Zodiac
of
magenta Aprils.

———————————

Wild poppy pain.

———————————

Beige lace falling down
&
blemished buttons
Burning.

Hardcore jewellery.

———————————

Sachet sex Sue.
Lanolin love.
Talcum toes.
Powder puff.

I'll vet your writhing slit
FOREVER,

drinking
eau
sauvage
from
an

atomizer spray.

JURY VET'S SNAKE SONG

CERISE DRAGONETTE I have piled my heart.
Cherry blouse I will undo.
This way smoulders largely and I am with you in
TOTAL SIGNATURE.

Skanking rudegirl pull it off cool.
Strange typhoons invade
my boss
horn
&
YOU
blow snow
to
make the bed
a
WRECK
of storms.

Logdark naked, flashwing swift, blade holes, coloured
SHOOTS
grasp my rod &
HURTLE
all
the starres against
this
VARNISHED REDHEAD NOW!!

You carmine peach.
You burnished buttons.
Soak our meat in stream crests.
Frisk & roam.
Maid, I'll boss your
trench
&
kiss the curves
until
your salted headscarf
splits
with steam.

We'll gleam like thongs
& dovegrey
straps
on high-heeled
Bordeaux
shoes!

———

No pink clues
as
fuck seeds
dance
&
rage.

JURY VET LOVE ODE

Burning TOENAILS of Nefertiti,
yr digital gang
betray terror in my veins:
I sink
beneath leathered
strokes
of passion & dire fits
of jealousy.

————

What frail display! Calamitous
kissed
hydrangeas
do
little
to
reply.

O
precious rafts
of nylon
light,

sucked
&
blown.

———

Feathered women
are the
worst,
they FLICKER in the wind.

———

Love bossette,
hear my low prayer.

HEAR MY VERY LOW PRAYER.

Burn the venom from this heart.

Suck down the spanner flak
and Let me strike quimfolds Now.

———

Bone & Blade
&
Broken starres.

★ ★ ★

BE LOGGED) LOVED (eaten tongue, cudded, yanked
  over, nailed,
          crashed in, out of, detrunked, weeded,
           baked heavy, licked)
Occulist, tilth binder, clit swampee, dog hound bayer,
  undreamed,
     pilled out, underside velvet, fuck snot. She washed
       bruises,
  O river rinse her virgin body clean. Beck bubbles
    I pleaded,

       take the mould, pube lichen, pistol come, quim
        trigger fanny juice, dewy fern
        hair swifted, sex weaponry
        in her go root.

     YOU THE SHIMMERTEXING PEARL
     WITHOUTEN SPOT OR BODY BRUISE.

         She gold pelt pulled down
            somehows. Be
            SIGNIFICANT,
       wolverine & leathered, twice
         fondled Victoriana tent fold nighties
       like roots PULLED DOWN. Burned
       thorn
          sack
       we know. The rest is snow
       AGLOW

Saluting stars & eating shit earth.

SHE peewit. Peewee. Plover glove flame.

    Streaked Mane Filament.

    Red hair burning.

    Moss goes idiot.

    One bitter harvest only.

UMBER SLEEPWEAR & ALMOST BED STARRES. Silver
pleated hems & jade velour. SCARF
knotted in an atmospheric
ploughshare Kiss.

Vermilion fingers,
sunset leather
digit pressgangs
invade his running mind.

PINK SERGE BE
CUDDLED
&
BE KIND.

TOENAILS. Madfer. Carmine
sunburst & whitesock toes inside
cream sandal shoes. TUCKING
quilted bedroom undergown. (I WORE
a green carnation & the day
was Big.)

Feet religious.
SHOES, I AM ABASED.

Belvis in cardinal kid she strides.

Andante green suede looks ashamed.

Haver wineblack she strides & Smiles.

((INK LEATHER COURT SHOES ON VERY HIGH HEELS)).

Footbroach, strapped, milk beck, vodka
couch body: long-legged,
cross-thonged,
mustard green.

HAIR UP.
Hair parted
Hair middled on the side.

Varnished redhead rust woman hair blazing
on the wedding party
hotel lawn.

You the varnished curse. You the sin
sign.

Small heaven of grins & girls.

METAL HAIR
& the doors are closed.

JURY VET: IN VOGUE

CHARTREUSE blanquette, shirt lavender, frayed
mustard thongs. Brown heels on JOSE.
Blue heels on JANE.
Suedefur tunnels, elbow-clutching
lambswool pylons:
I miss you
now.   BLONDINGS
wept
cashmere, viridian xerox
DARK. Cooling
Jaguars & gold buckles
GLEAM.

Melt our pinksnow Sancerre clusterings, O
the toes are lethal wiper
blades, sweeping Lady Di
country casuals
beneath your Marks & Spencer
kiltpin sex.

BLACK & ZEBRA
twopiece on much-ribbed Chrissie,

full-stockinged
STAR.

I HAVE SEEN THIS FAR.

YOU MUST
  teach me all there is to know
  of
pinstripe boxjacket tuxedo woman's pillhat
  velvet waistcoats,
  &
  Cup Court Shoes.

CHERRY BERET.
RASPBERRY SHOES.
MADDER SLITFUN.

Tufted Indigo, you'd better
keep her body
warm.

BE CALM.
NOW SWARM.

1980 COLOUR GRID: CINNABAR JURY STITCH: UP
1981 COLOUR GRID: CINNABAR PERFUME WORN
BY SUE

woman car. female lorry of all delights. Her mudguard thighs.
  bonnet indicators blinking. fine
  suede trousers grey gabardine (cloudy) thick-lined
  AVEC BILBERRY SATIN: green wool
  stockings (If you are
deceptive fragility – YOU ARE!), brass eardrops, red
  suede cuffed
  winter boots. Add silver, lampblack leather
  court shoes

  ((mix duck egg & moss)) – *Rain trench*
  Rainjacket. warm
  lined lichen green
zipped &
buckled.   GOLD dropping
  chunky, clip-ons. Easy satchel. YOUR NATURAL

SLENDER WAIST.

This Harpie Queen's makeup flow. Her eyes dream. Her dry gin mouth lies.
Gamboge pink you've rubbed against in a long time.
Ribbed
(wool, acrylic flamingo two piece on xerox
Sue
shredding letters from a shredded
heart), torn,
let's go public, flattered in bedrooms & on
floors.

Red

piped detachable pockets, blood stroked nearly, more
DASH
than CASH inside yr wardrobe of jalouse
cullote
evenings, tweed
legs.

———

Crocodiling pleated fleshfolds. Filament bulbness. Stark
schoolchild stockingtops

I've never slipped clean. STARLIT BRAS
& shimmy lichen
gumboots (buckles
& studs).

QUILTED BRAND-NEW RAINCOAT'S VELVET BELT UNDONE.

Kiss her 1980 strongly-stitched pale shirt.
Love the Dirt.

She wore a kingfisher suede cape

& the added machismo of a man's big silver stretch strap Rolex

Which
tells
the

Time

On her Ankles of Fire.

OBSIDIAN HEARTACHE drapes her in a scarlet Blouse.
Punkititi Amadeus moanings
tipped with skin.
Mad weather bluesuede pumps of Thea Cadabra, metal
pink beads shimmertexing
Inca sprints,
patent lips Undone.

Deborah, peeptoed silverama bindings.

Maxine, courted maribou trimettes.

THREE BAR DIAMANTE STRAPPER
TOED IN TIME.

YOU ARE SURELY A SLAUGHTERMAN'S CLOG IN A
SECRET WORLD
OF RED SUEDE FLAME
tassel loafers
&
washable yellow Satin
batshoes!

Tossed applique mirrors glass.

SLINK, high-carbon soles.
V-fronted
Alicante piping she Strides.

Fake leopard skin
dream,
ruched heels
&
interlocking sunray
stitchings,
YOU
ONLY,
KEPT MY MIND ON

Damson
Edges slipped
&
pouring Rain.

Mouldy toecaps bring
me
Home to
footjam just

The Same.

———————

STOP PRESS. JURY VET DISMISSAL SHOCK. TRIAL ABANDONED.

ALL THE NICELY PLYWOOD GENESES & TENDER GREBES

sink sullen brows in spit pools. Gob
runs, pension becks & nauseating stream crest
waves
of life with you.
Copy wreckage, glue driblets pocking baby's face,

women I chased on the lawns of Albion.

ALL FAILED TO REPRESENT STARLIT BODIES LYING IN THE
LIGHT FROM 16 WINDOWS.

————————————————

Albion, your women wearing shoes.
Straps & thongs, shoulder
beads, pearl
dust, viridian eyeshadow.

I cursed her nasal whining uptight stinging snaps
of ultra-real.

———————

Strangers disease the hearte.

———————

Now
you're behind each
stupid hill
we'll

recognise the awful night
by

STARS ALONE.

★

I kissed my Errors as they came.
Sucked sick real.
Tears flowing on the bastard zero ground.
Snap, cool down, wind-up furnace
nights, chewed.

She undressed at dawn.
She kept her shoes on.

'I want your fuckdust children
if you want me to,
inside this carbon dress and
leather stocking
tops at Xmas when I left lovers
&
sank beneath each
footblood
sigh:

to you I CAME & COME.'

Pray to nothing and nothing comes.
Pink specs attack the dawn
delight.

And You.

If I cannot do it Now I'll do it
with Someone Else.

AND SOON.

AXEING bitchette, slight me NOT
when snowings bilious come.
Tears pour dreadful vinegar on
You.
So far, casual, putrid concrete
roadways, piling
mossgloves. Tinted, bending
forlorn gravelike
excellence, humming
lips & Tongues.

Simpleminded you have graced my Scissors
& still come clean.

Neck chains.

Blot
love
come
now.

Ankle fire. Foot & fingerflame.
Swear a chain you forge in life.

TO SEEK YOU NOW IS POISON SURE.

Thus you Say:

Fuck dots
grab the scene

& if you cannot

Love me now,

THE DISASTER IS PURE GREEN.

THE BULB OF YOUR HEAD SHINES IN THE STREET!!
Icey love woman, icicle, melting
dagger, chest water soaking
shirts. Blood
is what your letters say.

Fishy tongue brides
crippled into sight
of Thee: kiss each nasty limpridden
edition
of the Real.

Power heads glancing, eyelocked, secret violins, Mozart
swoops through rooms.

WE ARE *ALL* PRIMADONNAS ESPECIALLY WHEN WE
SAY WE AREN'T (SWIRLING)!!

Dawn telephone blistering, I
come back to you, snailchasing
slowness unsubscribed.

No council coalbunker for us Now
that we enjoy the palaces
of ULTRA REAL.

Hand in boot, & loving all the women
which you are,
NIGHT COOL.

I HAVE BEEN INSIDE YOUR OFFICIAL SCHOOL

TO REPEAT THIS LOW BEGGING.

Dregs we suck
to name the childe Gullfingers,
dehiscent peaching
fanny, pouring,
crawling,
&

SPURIOUSLY UNREAL.

114

FACING FAX: DOCILE ADJUSTMENT TO DAILY HORROR

Happenings come fast. Fat flows thick. Spew spews.
        Wheat porridge glue.
    THIN dehiscent fuckdust streams
        their eyes
  when coming pollen Sun
      says Yes I Love You, But
      Don't Be Bright.

———————————

Blessed suedefoam pollutes each hearty fugitive
      these cinnabar days.

———————————

Blackfeather plaguepeople on the bastard sill.

Bitter
    sallow
        bricks of lime
& suicide.

       Kill acid Brides.

       Comb her filthy hair.

       She was my Pride.

HER DEMOCRATIC RATHOLE MOUTH DELIGHTS THE GUESTS

        & DRIVES
    THEIR SECRET MUSIK SPARE.

        ★

STREETERS INTO RED

   BREVE ME BRYGHTE clean green pearl. Breve
     brine supercharging urchin spunkette
       dribblings into. All you
    drab caffeine mums-to-be.
Shaved pork elbows, cumridden bras
     & laddered leather. YOU

floordragged, roughened
by violence, bangled
tits & tots.

VIXENATED HORNON LIPCRAWL,
BLONDE & REALLY GINGERED UP.

Fingered Up
crawl. Do much of nothing life. Basement
nostril windows.

Bring my long-staffed pony, polluting filthy
gangness. TOUCHED BY, in,
bent over, creamery de la femme, overcooked
by women & worse. FLICKER
bints beyond recall.

★★★★★★★★★★★★★★★★★★★★★
YOUR STARRY CURSE
★★★★★★★★★★★★★★★★★★★★★

Pearlish lusting pawtracks
across this people chest.

TELL ME YOUR HIDDENNUMBERS.

Pauline, always kind to menthol strides on you.
Kissed each cherry footglove, tongue
available
to
tu.
This ws Floor Event.

FLETCHERED TH'ARROW IN YR TARTAN LIPS.
Drank fierce wine
from buttercoppes.

You pissed on my shoes and told me it's raining.

Such scripts du marriage

do Fade.

HER DEPE COLOUR YET WONTED NONE AS
STREETERS INTO RED. Mascara
Suzzy's cinematic face.
ALL THESE HIGHLIGHT STRUTS SO GROUNDED
NOW.

Your wet red Paris hair,
is a magazine of
full
& total hero's liberation.

Chanel. Estee Lauder. Clinique fumes.

Hen Spice.

Wolfing coverlust
combines

SAPPHIC, venereal, cocks
combing gutters running
fuckbloode: Titless &
manyloved,

ALWAYS you are ZOOSHING Up,
tinselized & ready for a ghastly
Bang
of sans culottes
in velvet west end beds
&
silken
Rooms,

YAPPING TORNCUNT STARLET BOUNCED
IN TIME.

Razorbill comes down
on me.

Mouth irruption brings you
to the sedgey plucking
Post

to
drink the

daggered poison

down.

LOVEDOLE BEANOS FUCK SUCH PRUDERIE ANGLAISE.
Jury vet speech cracked a wheel, Smoked
    Bahouth carmine Toenails, jumping
        wires cut yourfilthy sand.

    Mildew postcards from yr wildweed Hands.
        Burning meadows black.
        Cool divorce in rain.

    Loveglow lustfoot shan't, Not Yet.

      Gamey bedroom porn.

      Stitched ankles moan.

      RIDING RIDING ROCKSKULL LEAP FROM ME.

   Children not yet Made sing Bind my Secret Body

        &
      Suck to
      Death

    FALSE HALOES CAST ON THEE!

YOU WANT HER BROKEN WITH HER MOUTH WIDE OPEN
BECAUSE SHE'S THIS YEAR'S GIRL.

Frail apache, rue de la disco waif, let me part the Dralon
    curtains down across the vinyl cushions
      of yr Birth.   Shattered rouge tete, drenched
natural beauty bounties & Bunty annuals
      combined.   JET leather strapettes
skim her milkshake skin, blue lights
      jive.

      All your dirty looks, wife, all
   the well-read books. Now we KNOW how sick
      people move. Liberal crasstorn
    pussycat bleeding, I MISS YOU TOO!

TALCUM SHOES PLEASE, pollen Bras,
pinstripe bootees
& lorded cumsoaked fingerling. Dogshow
MADNESS woofing pallid sex. O nunnery woman
SO MONKISHLY TOUGH TOUCHING YOU
in the thistle bristle wedding bed.

(This game's no sweat.)

Purslane Pauline sticks a lip.

Your single body's a striking SOVIET!

SOCIAL WORK TODAY: JURY VET SCANS THE RIOTS

SHEW ME ANY TARNISHED PLACE WITH
REALLY CLEAN HEARTS.
You bent me to the maythorn blood.
You screwed me over, among the vlix and vine.
You scrapped my charts & sank beneath a tonguebloode Cry.
You stole my square of Albion and made
it sore and Sick & Cold.

You, lanced with fog, bunny claws, clover leaves
dance like clubbed skulls in
fuckdust dawns of plexiglass
and leather truncheon
MADNESS WROUGHT
BY THEE.

(Her sullen brooch
is quiet
by the snowdrop's
GLASSY FACE).

SO MUCH, SHE SAID, YOUR STARE IS
ROTTEN BLUENESS, AS IF A STARRE
GONE SICK.

SAMPLED THUS, SHE MADE
HIM TICK.

Coins du feu, bleak lovenests rainchoked, cul de sac
                    nettle kisses, thistle wedding bed
            bliss bleeding plasma Now, no problem
                    honey. Teenage pulseholes burning off
        each wrist
                when coffee comes at 10.

            Escape your looks and network books.
    Manila folders burning on her quiet desk
            with skinhead children eaten
    to the marrow bone,
                beyond the poxy dole queue grind.

    Squat your legs in pissfilled doorways
        when petrol bombs Come Down
            on Plastik Spastik Oxfam Tins

    & skyblue pandas burn and blaze

        in the stinking urban wind.

JURY VET'S ODE TO PASSION

bladed HABIT & lustre. Lithic
                tuff's a holy pudding
                        in yr tarred tray: no seek
    reward. Chanced, ugly, silence down each's garden
                cloche, si blonde.
        Outsnowed & casual, maythorn fingerbloode
                itch glass alive. Lies
            jerk his fools gold pen & FILES
                    of culling dark. WHICH NEXT?
    Dust, burned particles, bracken mindflow, paw
                grubbings, nose
            money, angled fire. Au FEU
                de la storming
        accusatory digit gangland feathered
                lightness
            clings AWNINGS. Sun & trees
                gone sudden
        Real.
                TIELESS RAINCOAT MONDAY, Shale
    Foot.   Swift curve, tea blender, plum.

Single tone of wrecks.
                                        She eats

        her sex. Armpits & trains.

            No heart. No bloody
        valentine. Shew
    yr parent key
  is death. Un
breath.

                    I BREATHE YOU QUICKLY.
        Lung stench lasts all day.
        ★★★★★★★★★★★★★★★

        Cave beasts shine.

            Awful gas.

    NAIL.

    ★★★★

  Maggot gleam!
    !!!

BE A NICE GIRL KISS THE WARDERS

ALL I WANTED WAS A BAG OF FUCKDUST IN YOUR
  KITCHEN DOOR.
        ALL THAT CAME WAS ANGEL SCUM.

  Clean heart, you hoovered me th'Other way. Valentine
            diseases, glue bodies, Bunty
                fallout honey pots: a nunnery
                    soaked in slyme. Pink Lane telegrams
                    piling
                UP in tampon pools. Yr sanguine theses
                        prick a bra. Brown Cuban heels
                on Karen, plain satin Nehru troos
                    on Viv – slack trax to the
        EVER OPEN DOOR FROM YOU.

FUN of pointed primrose toelength
shudderings.   Weed's temptation
   shunning petal blood. Gas necks
                    chive.

─────────

No victims when the Arm comes down

& OCEANIK MILLSTONES OF
ALBIONCHOPTHEDARLINGNOW.

JURY VET PEELS THE STICKY STUFF

CUMCHOKED WOMEN YELL/I STROKED A LIP/STIFF PEOPLE
MOVE.

Torncunt swandown fingerling on Wendy's fan.
 Dying breath from you cuts gassed-up fins
   WHERE WATER RUNS FROM COOL TO BLUE.

────────────────────

Shew me what to do when sex is glue.

────────────────────

Who wants to be a victim crushed by pumped-up dirty
          five inch scarlet heels
   in sight of sensible brown leather
             GARDEN
             SHOES.
      (a secret foreign Cruise).

                ! ? !

────────────────────

LIPS, vacuuming velvet urban bedroom
fringes, sucked for real her cumin-scented
       TOES' saliva Rim.

female Dagger's broken coppe.

Stinkbloode cancels sightless STARRES.

 mouth-stings punish Ankle Fyre

 from afar.

Her lunar blindness is a famous scar.

122

ALL THE MISTY ISLAND FERRIES CANNOT
FETCH YR FRINGE
TO ME.
Zipping neckleather, muscled
bumps
&
I
mean
You.

———

Love you tempted Tudor rose.
Ful Debonare.

SHEW me blacksuede
high
heeled milky
gamboge
fingers
gleaming vinyl
terror Dark.

STRUT VOICING CHEEKS & SWANS OF GOLD.

———————————

Silkstraps falling, cloud bint, talcum breastpuffs,
lavender ignition valentine. HEELS SLIT FUN.

Milkflake honeymoon scissors shred fat suits. Nimbus stank.

———————

TUNGSTEN LEGS SUSPENDERED. Braless panti
hose women
shitting squatlove brix.

Pistil sucking lemon sky DO IT NOW NOW.

Citric sex.

Give Do. Do Give & always Do.

PRESHUS JOOL.
———————

ALL THE NICELY PLYWOOD GENESES MOCK THE SOULE AT DAWN

Sweltering poupee varnished redhead you'd better Listen
to me Now.
You have had a mystic Shower
& I know you Have.
Instructions come quicker than.   take off unrobe
& bend before the wheatgerm mannish
boy
who loves you as you ARE.

Quim vibration clicked in time
to strike an axe
against yr log
where moss defends.

Deneuveing porn

Columbining nowhere beds go bullion bad.
Piano music in my heart explodes
with aubergines & kings.

Stupid thread sews you and alters every sleeve.

Now you have punished me
I will eat red stones.

LETHAL DROPLETS COMING DOWN

SMACK HER FACE O PEARLIZED AUTOMATIK
JUMBO PENCIL.
Lipstick traces
crowded then.

Salix bendings, rivers don't Run.

SPASTIC acts defuse unFlame.
Bakelite hiplength moanings,
smashed with milk.

Bells & bones & telephones.

Love me. Do it now Now. Startled
halfcup bras, blistering
toenail madness. Palamino
DAWN
STARcrusher.

RACKAROCK SKULLBONE SMOKING.

Vapodust.

STOCKING DUST FOR FIRE

FUL DEBONARE she glistered on the secret
carnal bed,
chenile wrappettes uncreased.
Mousse shadows her concealer stick.
PEARLIZED rose & suck loose powders.

Automatic tit mascara flows.

Fluid cheek brushers combine with redrust hair.

AMBRINE SOLO PRESSED I AM NO TANGO TOY.

---

raked storming cheeks with
Marjolaine.
Frozen cliffjuts scalped & frosted tourmaline.
amazing jumbo pencils for your
eyes.
Liquid amaryllis true earth ground.

PRESSED POWDER haunting woven face a finely Speckled Cloud.
Pouring tulip champagne rain
in vivid gutters made by YOU.

Hen fur fretted, human always, stealthy
high-heeled court shoes
Creep On Me: YOU

bathe in manmilk
sweat & cloudy come.

Tongueflames dwell
impossibly
in broken hearts.

Bastard Zero Decade wakes you UP.

Nectarine Nothing
will happen again
if we don't love.

Praline justice eats the childbeater

HOME.

VETLOVE: RYSES UP IN HIR ARAYE RYALLE

SO SMOTHE HER SYDES FAR LIT TO PUSH THE
POYSON DOWN & TANGILL ME NO MORE.
DEWYNE, fordloked luf-daungere
pryvy perle withouten spot
I cast a die at Thee. her maraschino cherry
hair, streaked, no CHANCE BUNNY
SEEKING SHADE, HOLLOW
hairless armpit sleevy Sue. Her
fargone flame. To stroke
this cumin-scented
Rim. Pistol
friglumps blocked, unanimous quimchick
tracing, slowtrain
redness coming miles
from stalk to lip
WHEN LIFE BROKE UP.

Tied it Then in secret bloodknot fury.

Lychgate wifery /sniff madfleurs/ gone sickbad.

PULSING POMEGRANATE SHOULDERS
SHIFTED SUZE'S BEDFLAK

Too many men when women leapt from cloven palace doors.
Crystal fucklust smothering, ash
tearings, windpinned pauline axes,
ankle talcum, bathroom suspenders stretching, digit
creamery, ALL YOU SAID & ARE
when silk slipped down.

STEEL I wish a breasted smoke from callous embers Gone.

Skank ponies drive.

First chic slingbacks.

Raincoat glebe.

Curled and cropped.

Boygirl.

Climb for body rain.

JURY VET TESTS HER MEMORY

YOU BREAK MY HEART & I'LL BREAK YOURS &
WE'LL BOTH APPLAUD.
WE'LL NAIL OUR STUPID SCISSORS TO THE FLOOR.

Hungry broken gin-soaked faces
spew the grit of Nazi laughter, when
muscles gleam & wrench the filthy sky.
No blossom comes. Snake boots spark
the bullet earth & die.

Swill the scum down sluices made by men.
Tear the cuff & snap each milky wrist
so bathed in stranger's
COME.

I'll never know their faces blunt & dumb.

Silk manholes ruched
with swollen fuckseed streaming
in her angel veins.

Love's a bruised knot to fix the strain
of loving Thee, where
I comb the velvet sky to set
me
Free

from poison which invades
each
pore.

Rain snaps
the burning quiet,
&
all
the
piss–filled
clouds

gather brimming at my brow.

PREENING SHEEN DREAM: VERONICA LAKE

TROUBLED TWOLEG CHERRY HEAD YOU LOOKED
ASKANCE
AND GASPED A PRUDENT YES
IN OUR VIRIDIAN STARLIT XEROX ROOM.

(Shampoo
dripping
from her
smiles
said
GET A GRIP)

Firecombing brightness on Estee Lauder lips.

Dryven out of erthe I sank a shaft.
Broken blood came
back.
Stressed matchings.

Tongueclucks burning when
you took my arm
because I was too shy.

We split a brace of quail & never laughed
TOO HARD.

You teased and brought me from
the Edge
of
NOWHERE REALLY FAST!

No need to look for further blys in all
the firefame.

Sleek petal on meteoric rocks.

Tight cocks
gathered
in salt sweat
drive
each

SURGE IN THEE.

ALL THE MIDNIGHT CHOSEN: JURY VET ON FIRE: GUY FAWKES, 1981

THEE WASP WITH NAKED FOTE STALKING IN MY
CHAMBRE.
THEE WHOSE BRITTIL DERTES ARE PINKSNOW
TOES PEEKING FROM EACH DOVEGREY
BORDEAUX SHOE!!
Thee nonsense crawl has slaundered love.
THEE BLACK BRUISED & REALLY CREEPING THING
INSIDE THE HORNY FYRE.

Thee for cutting paper now & weeping bintglove madness,
thee for snow.

Open-toed thee. Andy Pandy dungaree
Thee.
Tea grows dark as the blessed season folds.

Pouring salt on Thee.

ACONITE & DREADFUL BANE THEE THEE.

Thee skanking two-tone ponytail at six o'clock
on the
Habitat bed
Harassed lips in the trimcut morn,
O THEE RUDEGIRL PULL IT OFF COOL IN
TONIK FRECKLE DRESSES
&
BRING ME FROM THE
EDGE OF NOWHERE
REALLY FAST.

Thee bodysnatcher.
Thee raincoat.
Thee pink military.
Thee go-go.
Thee selector.
Thee fast-speaking woman.
Thee apricot bridesmaid.
Thee Laura Ashley wonderful.

THEE PURPLE SLIT & TALCUM TOES.
Thee ruched by stallion
seed staff.

Frill tease comings, kiss
winking cuffchunks
at the door
where we explode. THEE

whose bangles crush the root in
me.

130

THEE VELVET VODKA HIPS
SOAKING HONEYMILK
MOANS.

THEE WASP STING DAGGERING PULSING CELLS
WHICH
LEAP & START LIKE STARRES.

THEE QUIMFOLDS BURNING . . .

Tongue touching slits
Thee.

RAMPANT QUILLS & SIENNA FEATHERS FLAKE
ON SOARING THEE.

There is no end to Thee.

((This is She)).

High damage & midnight
fifteen
(Thee,)
for
this
is
she.

JURY VET

Started September 1979
Abandoned October 1981

Wild Knitting

Everyday, everyday, everyday, I write the book
ELVIS COSTELLO

1.   Beneath the worm's eye view people. The clubfoot
Giro trek. Brandlings lob mucus
from the sloping lawns of Albion. Securicor
I'm only glad to be off the dole blokes, dark
glasses staring
from redundant Albion Mills (Idle), all
the broken dollpeople say: Meat meat give me
meat, boss: Boss me
Up
or I go Bostik nostril
& totally Sickrude, need to be
ordered, regular fishcakes & spam
every day I write the book
the bad book. Join the army
of deserters, council estate dogs
shitting in the beck, rimless cars, porn
videos & snuff movies on the rental
get you in the out
tray
from bondage underwear
& the bluebeat skanking jobcentre. Fast

Yosser skullbanging is It.
Fuck me Pal
hve you seen his
Totally Wired
Face. It's a trough: brutality
mixed with blood.   2. Spring's

fuck all, tilth & seed, you hve to cut the grass, who
needs it?   It's just stuff. Stuff it, them.

Rockstar posies, rubbishers
of text, the bowtie number
over Chablis, how rather sweet,

muddlers on a scheme, cashgrit
grinding you Out, Access cards
pouring, cars without gear trouble,
hairdressers & boutique pimps, take you

on a skyroute, dress like them: poptops colour up
    the kids, the Ripperkids. Stick to the guidelines, Pal,
    I'm the Govt's friend. This'll do that
    for you, one day. Blow down

        the jelly Jobcentre & join the nation
        of deserters
        at the Falklands, page three has it,
        join the Startrek Crew. Spandau Ballet
        on a council tenancy, screw
            the inmates.

3.   Bidet sundries crane the lacqueur Sundays, more
        bloatedbelly Zulu orphans
           on the world about us, while
           you're banged in
    with Argie bargie beef & kraft cheese slices.

No use boss I want the freedom.

But boss, I want to bend & shuffle & be small.
        What do, boss, what do?

Madness in speech, 4. fuming cloudpuffs, all these moody
        Italian perfume ads, ponce clusters, tongueclamps,
    rant money, bent fivers, all the Christmas crackers &
        cubist cripples, spastix in the dollshop,
  looking for an Airfix head, zimmer frames, spina bifida
cages, cocktail sausage fingers beginning
      at the armpit, dialling
    the wrong number. The Samaritans are ALWAYS
    engaged.

    Lipcrawling lethargy, bombed out
        on the rate support grant, twitch
    time is over. Last year's dream gondola
    on a dream ticket, collapsed, badly
  furnished: you're still beneath
        the worm's eye view. Suck
      the dregs & cry. 5. Dans ma filthy poche,
fiendlips.
      I like your demolition style! Now I know

      the halt & lame. Yr incoherence
      is famous. All summer kneelings

gone, gone. All the sickbad fume smells
on the marriage blissbed, rank pillow sweat
& juicy comegum. You left
& took It
quicker than a lightswitch, trimmer
than a blade. All these
vast zeros I'm
a zombie to.

6.   Vengeance trails me like a wound. Your gold
reluctant ring snapping tight
like a sack on my face.

what begging, crumbs & wiped plates. I'm blinking,
feeling it, flecked
with your spit. Too much
hanky use in the riveted
livingrooms of shame. Vengeance trails me
like a root, from early tillering to third node! What sulky
bends & nascent gloom
the wife brings home
with lentil puree
on a stick
to beat yr frying head
& make you see SENSE, that biggest
of boys.

Squaw madness dries me up. Deathdread
& beatblood, the wife
in word tumult.
You're silence, postcard quiet, no STD, many
flat ways. No stacking me, queengem, no
swoops or stems, liplap thrillers
redundant Now.
Just dullface, trillbone. You unmoved, you
the final monument to stillness; brief shimmer
breezed & lovely zenith. Cenotaph
of girls.

7.   We fiend blather. We rubbish wading. We far tracts
We timeless hopings, me rather. Macbeth quotes,
Who's Afraid of Virginia Woolf,
psyched fury, never papering
the nursery, none of It.

I wreck the cot & cuddle corner in my head, burn the children,
AGAIN

absolutely exiled, back on sentry duty,
   looking for a skull with dreams inside.

8.   Albion, you're just a bruise, steamy day wreckage.
      Wound, far penetration, sickness on my gentle sleeve
      Albion, broken down, Albion every day
      I write the book, this dark book, the wild book all
        the people lurch past my frosted windows,
        creatures
           & clones. I seek yr bones
           & desyre

      whatever touches you
         can lend me
         Now.

everyday I write this Book, Arcadia defunct, Albion
      sucking up to the calamity, wrenched from harmony,
   harmonie, broken keys, the personal manner of it, cash
      guitars weeping, totally
   cost effective madness, writhing blisses, wordblocks
      jamming the entrance, choked single moves, back to
souptins, individual mail & midnight flicks.

   O Thee, Thee, feather, holding it All in yr frail fists
       and lips.

Festival of boos, you triumph now. 9. Your hair a flag
   I would surrender to, but you're too real. You're
      serration, the torn flap. No swoops here
     but the biggest glide to Nowhere. Can't leave.
     Won't. Stubborn shoetoe pressing earth. Cannot
    reduce to.
      Can't skim. Promise. Me did. We.
        Where is it, you. Bless me
    without boss thoughts
      when I bend for pat
       or hug.

   Always bless & Do. Wrap me in fantastik kiss crusts.

You the wronged woman. You the complexity. You the seeker
     of buses & trains. You the wandering wife far from
     home.
    You beneath the curlew-whooping sky, sinking
      in my northern arms. Dimming forest of touches
       blest with Real.

We blister & blush
& Rush
for the nearest
Exit
now that Love's
tied knots
in her
straight Laces &
gone
right back
to
Mum.

pale shimmer in the kitchenette: 10. Deadlines
bang me & the phone is hell. One day
I'll disconnect this tinkling
red fucker. That will be that, Pal. Down
in the Stuka hole
all the whistles blow
at once.
Naff it, cool blade,
I'm with you
in the mintbed
beside the peachy feel
of sheep.

Or hot Hannah's torchlit invasion
where I blow smoke
& Never say Pardon Me
for being Quite Alive, sweetheart, let's
call it a night
& day.

It's like that, family drill.   11. Fury hits the kitchen,
on the rotten dark stairs. You smashed the china
& I froze in fear. Between tea & sleep
I rage & rave.

I imitate the shoe.
I walk miles under pressure. It is all too hot
for this gentle day, tryst & balm.
12.   How I miss touching
lines of care
along yr open face. Sickles
striking groinwards
in my sleep
are only part of It: I am with the spell

and there is no hope there.

136

What hisses from your lips is love under fire. Terror
of the hammered heart. The very carpets
are alive with feare. Trapped
in withering crosstalk, how
we may find this, that.

Only the harmless ankle
shews where we might be:

Give to this, & make no fluff: I love you.

14.   I was zeal, and zeal's troubled brother, miles away.

Slap me. Belt me like I know. Get me saying bossboss.
Get me bending so you know me Best. Tie me
stuff the word control. Right in me.

I'll confess: love's a rope, a firmament, deep trouble,
larking kisses, fast moves, sluggish attachment,
shared rubbish, psycho links, frustrated
amazement, Sex Pistols & Sibelius. A ring,
partial rigid stances, fanny glue, pony discharge,
all of it is a rack and a bed pouring with
money and vows. I'll confess
my scrapheap head: all I know
of pigs (sussex gilt), red mite flea, Jacob
Sheep my first wife went off with, brassica champs
for any village show. It's all here, blood
& rime. I'm writing it. Each ligament
snapping a fullstop Halt. Keep me
out of control. Fend me off. Unplug
my amps. Snap my wires, puffed clit. Feed me
sandwiches crammed with lichen, fursoil.

Here. Here! all my knowledge of buttersoft beige
kidsmooth sandalettes of Enzo Albanese & all the
Sparked Up peccadilloes in Paris & Bordeaux.
Hotbank Seine summers with celandine salad.
I only wanted to come home. Listen, I'll jazz it:
The high-heeled crewette, tie-dyed hair (scarlet
bouncing black), flared minds, chunky
pearl drops, marigold slipons, pale
shifts & Estee Lauder lips. Wild poppy blusher,
pencilled eyelines, Chanel lapping the couch,
reckless lace & gin, face pax, do you want me
do good. Do you? Making the place clean. Hoover
my head for once, clamp it, cull the shadowline,

beyond the edge. Not living off choirboy
sex probe with vicar/ disturbing revelations
that/ workshy teenager who/ stage struck sex
queen vowed today/ all the page three rumour
gang!

Her grinning the best of girls, 15.
sandals with another meaning,
tiptoe touches, trimlined pumps, pencil
heels, Chinese jadeyellow eyebrow blusher.
Mascara honeytrix and syrupmilk means,
court shoes bathed in human breath.
So close to death
& the cover of September Vogue.
Always a September girl.

Drink it. Down, down, how we do this, framed.

Stripped & torn, we're back
on page one. Ravaged
in the corn, strong men
belittled by doubt, I'm borrowing
your key
towards a future of loathing
now that the sky
is a blue desert,
starved of love: we go for the
ruched field, fantastically
liprouged, zest for fire
and the penalties
of speech
& blood.

this State of the Nation bulletin for Lesley MacSweeney
April–August 1983
Bradford.

RANTER

(1985)

for Lesley

Ranter

Ranter loping
running retrieving
motoring chasing
her with a cloakclasp
sniffing the trail
loving wanting
eyes on any horizon
but this blind spot
leaping the fence of his enclosure
nose down in open fields
stunned with blood
trailing her scent
greyhound quick from his trap

Moaning: *this must be the last lap*

And it isn't
even the first

swooping aloft
skylark on Skye
swanning around
gliding over glades
snipe drumming
stealing into empty nests
shimmering in hillhaze
Cheviot to Killhope Law

Ranter's folly
time and again

flouting the law
of averages

less than he started with

more than he bargained for

Ranter. Call him Leveller, Lollard,
his various modes.
Whispering sedition, libel,
love-lockets of memory
coaxed from his brain box

Whispering *I love you I need you*
to the stone in her
the still stone in her pale blue water

Fox she saw
in Manchester snow.
A winter flame, she said.
Red as a heartache
pumping through him, flourished
like a rose
before her
at the dream station.

Another extravagant example
another project running over budget.
Men in the know
chewing ends off cigars
eyes rolling to heaven
over Ranter's back,
where he mewls alone,
barking: *The luxury of punishment
is breaking us all.*

Ranter the straight man
replying: *I know, I know.*

Ranter: Leveller, Lollard,
Luddite, Man of Kent, Tyneside
broadsheet printer,
whisperer of sedition,
wrecker of looms

feathered and peltstricken
bound with skin

hung up in trees
Bamburgh to Canterbury
wasted on the ground
alone in his slurry bed

Ranter mashing his teeth

chewing over memories
of her with a cloakclasp

Picking up Bede and Cuthbert
on the ham radio
in his birdbrain wolfskull
wondering why they don't answer back
wondering why Sweeney hasn't called from Killiney Hill
above the gentle shores of Black Rock

all too busy keeping famine from the door

Halfden's longboats
ploughing the shore
Bamburgh at bay

Newcastle gets ready

Men of distinction
in the chapel yard

Ranter roped up
hurt in him
heel on his neck
Halfden's heel
under the Raven banner

Hadrian's leather boot

militiamen
academy-trained
or the swinish from pubs
clubbing his door
with butts

Ranter reminded
of blisters and boils
hurled off the causeway
asking for Bede

Salt.
I got salt.
Asking for Aidan
I was shown the shore.
More dismal dismay
for me and my fiefdom.

Aching for seawind taste.
Sky's forever moving, spindrift
dazzling when sun gets through.

Thrift like a haze.

Learning silence of cells,
moon through the slot,
prayer power in the dungeon
of his life.

Nut-brown brothers
with earth-browned hands.
Nets and psalters
laid down for the day.

Aching for breakers
breaking his monotony,
sick on the boat
to the island he loved.

Norsemen used to it
life on land and sea.
Maker of maps,
gutter of towns.

Bamburgh to Bewick,
eye of the island
in flames.

Forsaking the dunes
dune misery
stranded on the strand

monks
organising
the next page of Codex
from a cell

driving himself
out of the wild

Returning, returning
Ranter searching for the good thing
the place with a centre
inside her cloakclasp
lignite and beryl

sweeping up her generous plaid

hoping she will utter a good thing
giving him reason
to turn and return

without pus-pillows
burst on his back
chin
cleftsmote

heart a stranger
to the good thing

Gifts and bounty
on the wedding feastshelf
unwrapped

none taken up
all of these days

none of them opened for more than a year

Dear God
what kind of country is this

reduced and reduced

cloakclasps exchanged
braid-pins and pipers
straw men attending the feast
fipples, fiddles and bows

smaller than the word for small
smaller than the French word
the Irish

smaller than the smallest word for small

Ranter ranting:

Where is my bride
holy of holies
Curse on the weather
for being so straight
and everything else bent

rubbing stubble
on his wolfchin

Cambridge fenfields
burning up summer
without her

Ranter the wanderer
Ranter's bride
walking the Weald:

Pilgrim's Way.

*

God, give me strength

What kind of country
People wearing shoes

exercising the cheek to breathe
cheeking the Law

Lollards, Levellers
Upside Down folk, Miltonic upstarts
heroes & heroines
reading Shelley
taking up Anarchy like a pen

and Ranter

on the run

running and running
remote and reduced
reduced and reduced

Pelted with feathers
in his other life

One third
in trees.

Word for reduced
word for running
word for betrayal
word for bond
the one for moving
for fast

rocking down
the Dartford Loop Line

Ranter away with himself
broken and broken

running to Lee

where she clouted his head with stones.

*

Lord, Lord,
Bede is your servant

Let me be his.

A whole day without her.
Two.

Three running into four.

Scratching them off
in his cell.

Grief.

Word she used.
Now it's a badge.

No one to touch in this risky business
moving and moving

chasing her across lawns of Albion

Ranter's record
filed to copy:

Ranter, I said.
Call me Ranter.
Name woven inside
this cloakclasp.

This is my power:
To peck and roar.
To be feathered,
furred and fanged.

To hunt,
sky above him.
Grub-hunting
earth at his feet.

Feasts and pipers,
dogs on the moor.
Allendale's princedom
running with streams.

One third in trees.
One third heather
stalking
the sheep's track.

Trout only
surpass him
for swiftness
up streams.

Hunt
fly
hover
howl
harass
wheeling in air
alone on his rock

Then I am a man.
One third, warming
the fipple.
His flute song.

Upright to earth
this dear green land.
Clouds go
where I tell them.

Bolt-holes of memory.
Harmony with Kes.
Badger reads me books.
Good old Brock.

The rest is skin,
gun at his back.
Surviving in houses
broken by marriage.

Warlords with clout
at the rim of his princedom

*

Listen Cuthbert.
Come in Bede.

Your time's up
I need help.

Aidan
where are you?

This is Ranter calling
on VHF.

Halfden's heel on his neck

grubbing for lugworms
Druridge to Dungeness

Tide pouring over
causeway he loved

Ranter revolving
riptide of his life

My fingers cannot
grip the limpet shell

Kelp on his ankles
Crabs gathering in silent gangs

Crown and cloakclasp
soaked in saltflow

Kilt in pools
sucked by elvers

Dear Christ
my eye is put out

Eels mating in his hair

word for bruised
word for banished
words for forgotten victory
word for psalter
words for slowness in her
none to be said

Vespers lost
brine pours over

broken pustussocks
soaking chestchin

Ranter not giving in

*

Ranter, Ranter
shew us

Leveller, Lollard
what do we do?

Say this:
Go to the fields
make hay while sun shines

when it rains go anyway

in the goldstook meadow
afraid of sickle and stranger

villagers of Reeve
beating with hammers
straw and wooden
effigies of Paine

until
their hands
ran with blood

*

Dear Christ
what kind of kingdom

People standing in the fields all day
in the rain
doing nothing
leaning on sticks
glaring, miserable

resentment filling
their chapped bodies

afraid of everyone

and themselves

flexing wolfmuscles
feathertips turning
snipe drumming
gin-trap sex
climbing above her
clamping in loveclasps
dog in his rage
vixen in heat

*

Ranter, Ranter
glory and light
wisdom and fount of wisdom
bringer of beck water

climber of Killhope

law unto himself

picker of rosehips
conversant with Brock
swooper with Kes
dispenser of fortunes
terrible plain speaking

distiller of bilberries
smiter of spar

loper, glider,
dashing for game,
loading his gun,
cleaning his blade,
trap setter, marriage-breaker,
reader, desperate for attention,
bruised and mighty,
strangler of cries,
particularly his own
driver and driven

moving across this dear green land

hunting her with a cloakclasp
curl in her hair
in the nest of her family
brooding

and all this:
trembling, touching,
feasting and famine

*

Ranter's diary:

Particularly lovely
lee wind
ruffled her garments
Deptford to Woolwich
handsclasped
remembered her praying

air she was still in

staring
into the green courtyard
of the poor people's hospice
in Woolwich Old Road

Boats for pleasure
Boats for war
bobbing on the tide

Isle of Dogs
he ran with fangs
barges for bridges
across dry docks

fipple bent
in his creased beak

singing:
make me a blackbird again
not a groaning man

no collar on him
no family ties
but ring of blood
sweat circles
on featherpeltskin

watching his own
winding-sheet
and the smooth water
its sad envelope

as he touched the hem
of her life

Below the Yacht pub
Ranter writing
with a stick in the mud:

My whole life pulp
Brock wouldn't touch

Waiting for Sweeney's
Irish misery
beamed in from a bough

Howth to Sandy Cove

ham radio

ham-fisted
wrong-footed

Beak to phone
(feint crackle):

I am in a burned-out building
Powerscourt House
fighting weeds
in the Japanese water garden

I have returned the architect
to Versailles
with his glass ideals

I have ordered the turning off of fountains
in the Alpine park

floodlights dimming

lights going out
Black Rock to Louth

giver of feathers
to Agincourt fletchers
arrows bedded
in the emerald sodpark

alone in my bonsai
reduced and reduced

feathered slave
to unreasonable demands

*

prayer in peltchest
where are you love
psalter protected by wings
keep me going, Lord
plaid laid by pipes
My feast, brother
palace of his making
My house, keep out

Lord
to be called lord
prince
standing right in a princedom

fisted vigour
and prayer
Cuthbert busy
with Codex
and the travelling flame

Howling at the stone in her
beak-songs
he lapped her edges with
he winged her water

the lost darling

words and letters
drifting on the wind

four for the condition
six for her name

*

tracking the spore
Charing Cross to Lee
last train down
the Dartford Loop

station blacked out
like Ranter

tripping, falling
down subway steps

welter of blood, sick
lost luggage in his fury

chin cleftsmote
blood matting feathers

music hall routine
key in lock

Stroll on, Bill
where's me eyes

Who nicked
the lightbulb

Who pulled down
the permanent blind

Ranter upright
on the sofa

Bloodcake shirt
vomitbib drying

Courtesy of
London gin

Ranter
the lurcher

living in a friend's bathroom
head intermittently down the pan

feint flush on his cheeks
spew-syphon in his beak

*

waking: This is not possible

*

Ranter
torn from his trust
threshed & broken
down in the granary
cracking pods

Rhiannon
black lambswool plaid
twinklefeet
turning
kidleather shining

striding
rock to rock
wanderer

never chain her
to family stones

she spat in my face

dewy nipples
dried in defiance

larking sunlight
caught her hair
black
as dragon breath

Breton madness
lighting her lips

fleetfoot Diva
showing quarter irons
sparking flint
above Ranter's handwave

body and soul
a budded rose

ready to be opened
by kings

*

Ranter's children
driven out
by D'Aubigny
foster fathers
for orphans
driven on by Mobray
Durham to Evesham, 1069

Ranter's head
carved and set
beneath volutes, 1075

on the voissar
scratched on his neck
ROBERT MADE ME

grooved snout

separate from other men
women too high to touch

in 1100
I was a silent watcher

eight men hanging
at Bury St Edmunds

ropes and rings
knotted over pegs

gallows-man
in a scarlet gown

ruddy slippers
and black hose

pink fleurs de lys
invaded the psalter

1130
St Oswald's, Gloucester
I slept for a year

and woke
winedrunk from day one

drinking from a costrel
from hostel to hostel

hating the French words
invading my books

driven out
by the wife's dark looks

kicking dust and traces
with Wulfric and Harthacnut

jabbering Saxon verbs
the poetry of battle

blood on the words
which are Northern

Writing: *I am Eadwine
Prince of scribes*

*

Shivering primrose
and the wind's dark beat

down his tunnel
Ranter's grooved beaksnout
glowing in the dark
dark of his making
changing frequency

Ranter. Mad & brain-sick,
Captain Pouch, Plug rioter,
verb for rising, knotting ropes
in Spithead, offering wrists

for chains

slippery digits
in his oily duvet

banged to rights

shimmering rape
and the heart's dark beat

And Ranter's bride:

disappeared
over every horizon
praising civil disorder
singing for the sleepless

Chaucer in her lap

*

Ranter the leper
sheet on his back
hedgerow kingdom
ditch den rain
hole he sprang from
scattering stones
his head burst through
perforated eyes
shooting bloodleaks
noseglove squeezing
through the gap
arcing, twisting
punching grasshumps
rolling in rosehip
flaked on flags

teeth buried in clover
fists in thrift
pollen on eyelids
more gold than gold

bell on his neck
bell of her leaving

from the aching hole
flopped on the ground

bootless, without fable
molars mincing tilth

broken like he should be

Snipe Drumming

alone on Ranter's Rock
gull-smeared woolsack
lochtide sunblade
falling to the far shore
under McCleod's Table
like Ranter
exhausted with bringing light

Resentment
rising like liquor
pity of her silence
in little rooms
she made life
part of their neatness

No big swoops, she said,
in a fragment
in the village he loved.

snipe drumming
Ranter's wet head
turning
inside the noise
Snizort streaming to saltwater
at Skeabost
Ranter diving
out of the sun

snipe drumming
Ranter's Pool.

Otter.
Liquid like them
revolving
running windburned
refugee in exiled fiefdom
ewe-skull
picked from a ditch
bare to the bone
stripped by predators
endless wind
under the furnace of heaven

Ranter's cot
under eves

Ranter's bride writing:

Mill chimneys and derelict sites,
burning rubbish in back lanes,
high moors of mist and snowdrifts,
to the land of Bloodaxe and Bede
you fetched me from the city I loved.
Kiln-bricks piled high in a yard.
Men with flushed faces and women alone,
children scratting from door to door.
Families gathering in silent gangs.
I knew city sparrows and riverside
pigeons. You shewed me the curlew
in a far-off place I didn't like much.
The people or their guttural tongue.
Their sudden warmth disarmed me.

Woman of shame
lover and friend
silence until autumn
when we may meet again

Drumming the wold
my man
wielding the world.

How you can
do this to
me I do

not know. A
woman of shame
it comes easily.

My family &
friends. Summer
joy

without burden
of loving
you, adrift

on riptides,
anger and spleen.
You were drunk.

I didn't like
it much. No swoops
in me.

Now I'm here,
river
I love.

*

Ranter beneath The Plough,
Taurus, Orion, starring
a universe of chaos
hiding her with a cloakclasp.

More harpstrums than kisses.
More refugees than guests.

I travel in the dark
so you won't know me.

*

This is hopeless.

Flexing
at field's edge,
body at home
in this country,
small baggage
of history
flickering
between us
like the film
it is.

A lost world.

*

Skull teeming danger signs.
Ready for your wildest attack.
Seek wisdom. Would go to some
great man if I could.

Halfden or Bloodaxe or Bede.

Taking my hammer and books
leaving you alone.
Using my blade to furrow
I wouldn't be happy.

Would long for the long cry
as the prow bit your sand,
flailing villages into welts
of widowhood. Blood on my blade

in rosehip and fern.

Time for books after the scourge.

Sit in my cell with a quiver
of pens, gold-leaf for the page.

Drawing maps, borders
wanting more than I had.

For wisdom return to myself
wearing pelt because I am wolf.
Wolfric my brother a hearty man.

Killed with my axe
and now he is in me.

I am not always stone
at the end of your
accusing finger.

But when I am
it is flint
for pruning & plunder

Thor's thunder
driving my arm.

Ranter's Reel

Phantom, phantom
bringer of dread
smiter of spar
head-tosser

cross-burner
drunk from day one
lolltongue wrapper
around any bone

the one of contention
bloody love battles
splitting her crystal
to smithereens

cheekpouch stormlord
billowing plaid
thumping his breastbone
grinding his axe

Saying: *Look out*
every scattered atom
on the dire pathway

And Ranter: *They're*
all behind me
lost on the moors

but she isn't

Crawcrook to Consett
the red desert

Wylam to Prudhoe
Bunting and Bewick

Corbridge to Hexham
pearl of his princedom

Catton to Allendale
hunting for meat

Rookhope to Dirt Pot
tunnel to tunnel

Hollywood Charlie's
to the bend in the beck

Dove Pool to Allenheads
one mile in sleet

Fir Tree to Stanhope
boarded up schools

Alston to Nenthead
and back

greasy lustre
of surface fractures

back to his beck
stream for bathing

laving his back
broken by loping

from hedgebreak
and beck level

pinebough to pooledge
turned from his track

snared on the fell
beaters with sticks

county men, stocks
at their shoulders

snouting hounds
falcons on traces

hounded and hounded
midnight attacks

pebbles through windows
flogged in fields

for breaking a hoe
and answering back

Worming down
tunnels
of history

Ranter setting
his date: 1349

Blackheath, Ranter's
proposing place

date of his emerging

so kept under like beasts

Recording on a slate in the rain:

Give me your hardest hardness
your bitterness, your spleen
Give me the harshest harness
thrown off by beasts used to your harm

your inability, your dreadful shame
your words untouched by human warmth

all liquid innuendoes and brittle salutes
quartz-tongue flint-heart, pass me
jagged qualities of your meanest acts

Your silence beginning with O

Broken stiles
littering the princedom
neglected ditches
clogged with clarts

locked-up chapels
where lamenting starts

sheepwire stapling
her fells and fields

wild Northumberland
hemmed in, stitched up

more dismay
for me and my fiefdom

Up in the crow's nest
beak in a twist

Shrike talk:

I'm black grouse. I won't fly.
Ptarmigan, one of the beak mob.
You can't beat me up
I'm a big bird.

My heart a harvest
keep your threshers at bay.
I won't have Massey Ferguson's
rolling over me.

Stick your agrarian plan.
My body a soviet
but I'm not yours.
I'll fly free.

I'm a beast of burden
I won't move an inch.
When I'm not zigzagging
I'm a stick in the mud.

I'm a growler not growling
not doing my job.
I'm the hound with a dark stain
chained up in your yard.

If I'm to be whipped
then whip me now. Kill me
first, tied to a handrail
in the filthy street.

Smashing my knuckles
with a walnut gunstock
so I can't pay you back.
Drawing my claws.

You'd better do it
because I'm butcher bird
lancing my foes
on hipthorn and may.

I'm red grouse,
pride of the moor.
I won't flit
this hole in the heather

because you say so.
Heaving bags of rubbish
by moonlight, dragging
the family cart from door to door.

Won't lie in duckdown
when there is bracken & slurry.
Wander the fellsides
rather than be used by you.

You're Boss Lip
brass in his pocket
and a brass neck

Titled Lord
but I'll tell you this:
this is my princedom
you're on the wrong ground

And this:

I won't lope
I won't fly
I won't run away

this is my palace
I know every bolt-hole
better than the veins
on her back

Cock pheasant in my head
ploughed field my cockdom

Snipe drumming
egging on daughters
to mischief and vice

Magpie sucking eggs
until you're broken
begging for friends

Furrow
or fiend
depending on the weather

Wound
you haven't seen coming
the birth of pain

Mighty Leveller
one you thought resigned
to books

Phantom of distress
with blooded axe
and a fiery role

Shot from a Range Rover
I will rise

Freed from neck-chains
walking in your door
armed with centuries of anger

Friend
your wife admits
when you're away

Family and animals
in the grip
of my cunning

Vet
with the secret stare
a secret injection

King Digger
your burial
first on the list

Prince of Lollards
with the very last libel
in every parish
beneath your shoes

I will be back
again & again
you won't know how to rest
who to say to:

Get them seen to

Your chances
thin.

I have seen you
and never forget a face.

Had better do this:

Lock the doors
check the latch
eyes on each sash
it's all you've got

Damp the fires
put out the light
look in the thatch
for a flaming brand

Listen Pal
Compadre
Colleague
Friend
Listen Dad
Lord
I know thee

you've had it

Check your children
in their pink cribs

Watch for the tinker
at the turn in the road

grinding scissors
to trim their hair

I've a headful of blood
and your daughter's next

Your seed has reached
a dead end, Lord
you're washed up

end of the line
for you and your breed

You're a marked man, master

Death's drone
at your door

Final shudder
final fling

Final chant
from the last piper

Your future & fiefdom
down on my dancecard.

Flamebearer

Torchlit smoulderer
one with the light
hell-raiser
hunched under McCleod's Table
scorched with his own heaven
Scald scalded
dancing in embers
fanning the flames
of his own destruction
Ranter's furnace
sealed & shaking
head-bursting pricks of heat
light like sun
flaring

waking from sleep's apology
aching for some portion of chime-talk
beautiful commerce
she traded in

Ranter
burning his boats
blowing his bridges

oil from the buttress
poured on himself

ringing his own bell
Quasimodo

tracing her melody
in the flight of birds

the misery
of an embrace

pity of the little creatures
inside her head
lurking behind the lace of memory

Lauding: *King Fool*
black horehound crown

axe and hammer
raised to a skull
hammering home
Ranter's brand:

home from the war
of loving her badly
back on my own ground
blade in your heart

Albion ablaze with winking stars

Ranter
flamebearer
prince with a torch-song
five years on the edge
lip of despair
one on the brink
drink to drink
sting to the enemy
smoothing his honey
toast of the tribe
drinking:

Lord, Loverde
I cupped the roses
in her kitchen garden
scented sweetness
from the dark of a lair

heat from her body
set me alight, Lord
I was a match
for her flair

she was kindling, Lord
wet grass in the morning
her body on fire
with a singular parting

Lord, listen
we wriggled and writhed
sang in the sheets
my blade in a tree

moving quickly taught us
the art of flight, Lord
climbing mountains
to the heart of her glare

an explosion of wills
a beating of fists

Writing:

smell of stock
I was invaded
God protect me
where I stand

*

I saw her dandle
with a man and his money

twined together
beneath the mustard moon

night-scented she was
hungry and broken

her life a fuse
of fragile devices

Lord I was in her
and it came to nothing

she dawdled and dandled
climbed through his hair

heart-crushing joy
forlorn estrangement

all that was spoken
all that was broke

Lord I was beneath her
and it made no difference

glinting pendilae
hems to be kissed

Ranter's lip-fever
the touch of a ring

buckled angel
under northern storms

Lord, I was abased
abashed by her beauty

bending any vow
in the heat of a moment

sleeping like strangers
scorched by sin
addorsed and affronted
begging for more

pit of the stomach, Lord
shaft and trench
freed from its lock
the flywheel whirred

Listen Prince:
she walked her bitches
all over the meadow

eight fingers
two thumbs
on every hound

howling and growling

harrows and heel-ploughs
breaking the back
of land he loved

*

suivante she was
privy perle withouten spot

doucement duckdown
they bedded in

Suibhne stroking
his dream of Siobhan

unhooking her bra-clasp
in several great cities
and one Quaker town

Ranter the peacock
armed with strut

*

Ranter's bride
bird in a cage
banging the feastshelf

Seething:

Then you wore me out.
Stone at the end of
an accusing finger,
flinched at your fist.

Salt-block
rasped by a tongue.
Your tongue,
prince of my dithering.

Now I'm a tree,
my own patient roots.
Freed from you,
thin in the wind.

Dockleaves dancing
in the dawn
and autumn rain.
A stone alone.

Wind in a tree
that made me
what I am: mad
and stone-lonely.

Scorched by August
in that foreign place.
December excluded
from the songs.

When bilberries darken
you'll remember me,
blinded staring into
your labradorite eyes.

You the bloody warrior.
Helmet-crusher raised aloft.
Foulmouthed blade-breaker
on freezing fells.

You prince of pipers,
pride of Sparty Lea.
My fingers brushed
your closing lids.

When I kissed you
the dark was a torment.
You fetched me
surges, deep like a sea.

Sad I was, sad: mad
like a dog. Bitch I was
away from the pack, and
you my discreet lover.

My body the smoke
of hill chimneys.
I'm whirring
like a flywheel

and you won't
know me. A wafer
your rivers
flaked clean.

You can lap against
my absence forever,
beat your wings
in the dark of my leaving.

Alone on a crag
when you joy to the peewit,
remember I left you,
unhinged my dandling hand.

When you crouch alone
in the pillars of grass
broken by moonlight,
remember, rabbit-catcher,

the curse of anger
is in you. The shame
of fury and a harrowing
lust for control.

I wouldn't go with you
down that road. Now
we are both alone
by rivers we love.

You the prince
of beck and burn.
I watch the Thames
in my own quiet way.

Streams like blades,
slow tides and times.
We are all flowing
to a wider place.

I wandered and wandered,
wouldn't settle
in a place that suits.
Loved, then not for long.

When you glow in flames
of distant fires, remember
I loved you in hound's clothing.
Remember my prayers.

Please remember
I wanted above
all things courtesy.
In this you failed,

flailed me with passion
like grand punishment.
Whip of your love
became my traces.

You, jerky songbird
in hound's clothing.
Featherpeltstricken
moaning cloakclasp poems

even when I lay gladly
in your northern arms.
Haste is foreign to me.
I prefer to be slow.

Born under family blows
you will always wear
the warrior's ring, long
for the long cry

and your blade buried
and your heart on fire
with unpunished blame.
For you the wounds are real.

Ranter, love, broken prince
crowned with bracken by
bullies just like you.
Robed in the crystal water

of streams to ease your back
broken by loping, where I
forever pressed surely
loving to calm you

in the time of our trial.
See my scallop shell
and wild hermit shoes.
I lift my hem lightly.

Finnbar's Lament

God forgive me
least of souls

forgive my face
its crookedness

my heart sceptical
    searching for justice
in unexpected places

my scoffing tongue
    whose flinting
drove her away.

For offences
    in every princedom
let me offer this:

Persistently drive me
    down every lane
in which I spoke asides.

Hammer home my rudeness
    strike my head
confirming my badness

making most
    of my humiliation. Then shall I
thoroughly be bent

distraught in sorriness
    and woe
my unforgivable compleynt.

My heart alone an instrument of shame.
Let go Siobhan
to wander back with friends.

I will write for you without persuasion:
I did all this and more. I was an animal
unleashed on souls

more used to prayer and prattle
in the joyful dawns of breakfasting.
Break my blade. I will dance on its fragments

in any public place
you care to name. I will hop
till blood comes.

Then I'll write with fingers dipped:
your punishment is light enough
for all the mischief

Finnbar's done.
I have no slaves but sell the dogs.
I will take you to the kennels

and to the cloakclasp jar.
To the furnished nursery
but there are no babies there.

Take all the splendid plaids
in which Finnbar once held sway:
that's not a theft

to bother me, stripped as I am
    of delight & power.
Take this small but neatly-written

list of friends. For minor gifts
    and several brief encouragements
they will help compile

an index of my crimes.
    They don't betray. I am happy for their
willing talk to be unweaved

by men bereft
    of knowledge
inside locked rooms.

I accept your governing.
    Your tutelage
once made me

gather baron clans
    prepared for war.
But I accept it now.

Loot my sties. Prod each pig
    to market or the spit.
I'm done with feasting.

*

This is the chamber where it all came true.
    Strip the covers and sell the bed,
throne of our beginning.
Throne of love's dark days.

This is where she was, Lord,
    and I was master.
We drank from costrels
full-brimmed with wine.

We never had the ring of care
    beneath each eye.
She always had her things to do
and I had mine.

Listen, master of my punishment
    I am surliness defined.
I have never been one
to do the knuckling-down.

My native tongue delighted
    in the salty blow
of oceans in which
I splashed and sang.

I was a redshank lad
    in heather and gorse
with gleaming braid-pins
and her letters of consent.

Preferred my blade
    to the slow business of books.
You can't kill a man
with a word.

For these admissions
of course I do
expect an extra
stroke or two.

*

181

This is where I bathed.
This is where I never shaved.
Proud of my long hair, combed in the manner
which sent her swooning.

Bladebreaker Finnbar and swooning Siobhan.

And here is the psalter
and here the blood-fine:
I dragged him from a monastery
and made his spirit mine.

God, my holiness, justice
was a button to be undone.
Her buttons, Lord of my
terrifying punishment.

And here are the pipes,
architect of undoing,
here are the pipes
by the fireside laid.

Play the pipes
for my undressing.
Press me forward
to be flayed.

*

Here are the books she left by in a hurry.
The brooches and beads and the cloakclasp jar.
Her hurry to wander from lethal moments,
from the looms of slaughter built by Finnbar.

Here soft woollen garments which clothed her leanly,
the plover-green plaids for the honeymoon walk.
Here she almost wasted in confinement speechless.
Here she wanted for the slow tunes and easy talk.

For I was and am an haughty chief, used more to harpstrums
than slow breathing from a woman's lips.
I turned the filidh from the hearth and battle wrecks,
cut down foemen's heads from chariot wheels.

Who was my appledawn bride is now the plaintiff
sorely gathered in with her grievance deep.
She'll take me to the Judgement Mound
where for my offences many against the kindred

I shall rightly be impaled or strung by fires.
My own satires shall be turned against me, my courage
diminished, and magic gone from the streams and wells.
My own mead hall forgotten from the songs.

For this and all my other aches and pains inflicted,
apply your justice well. I expect the judgement:
to be driven from the tribe and to be denied.
To be belittled in the dust of my days.

Who was my bride in maythorn blossom days,
who was my bride from down the Finglas road.
Who was my bride the pride of Fingal's clan.
Who was my joyous love broken and gone.

Taut-cord-binder, leg-shackler, ankle-twister, knee-crusher
of mornings when I am vulnerable most, rack-winder
you alone are witness to the grievous loss experienced here:
my misery, brehon, dogs gone from the warm hall.

Listen, man: she hadn't done her best things yet.
Who was noontide clover-bee buzzing of days,
who was my bride. Who was gladsome gatherer
of seeds and stems in the nooky garden shades.

Who was the harbinger of pea-pod wine, noblesse oblige
who sometimes fixed her lips for queenly love-paint war.
Hark, stern one, when you have gathered your forces
and gathered me in, remember I loved her uninterrupted.

This is where we lay together, exhausted and true.
This is where we strayed beyond normal in the bedroom twining.
This is where we spent the peewit days in silence solemn and grave.
This is where we woke each day to a heatherglad beginning.

Those windless woodsmoke mornings, I wooed like a hound,
sniffing her traces. Jawking and lapping her laughter lines.
Harsh one, I was tranced by her magic stillness.
Your hardness-to-come, I would dance before her nakedness

and not feel the soul of my face burn like a brand
in an erasure of embarrassment for once in my life.
She weaved me, magistrate, to the tune of her willingness,
to the songs of her yesness, to her bosom of sighs.

I listened there to the little heart that pounded.
I listened to the North Sea in her stone-blue veins.
I wondered there at the whimsical mouse-murmurings
as her blood-ebbs turned tide with the moon.

Opening of her lids was like the rising of larks
in the blue slowness of a stubble-burning day.
She would stretch out her arms, disgrace-fetcher,
and I would lose my identity for hours on end,

displacing my power and delight in power, and my desire
for the wrecking of other men and the tormenting of tribes.
We would twinkle to the hearth, bearded one, and
wrap ourselves in the rags of our fortune.

Beast, she would purr, beast-enfolder, when I tickled
the physical appointments she treasured most.
O tip-toe she was to the water-butt for laving
those delightful cherishments, those little nut-browns.

And those breeze-bronzed curvings, and those angled
by bone paler because they do not see the sun.
And those tendons, designed by her long-hour stretching
of legs for the basket-gatherings when summer came on.

Quick command she had of shyness uncontrolled. Her
stutters were a charm to me even in the halted speech
employed by her to wave away my wanting. For her
alone I would desert the unsheathing of blades.

I'll never see another like her all of my days.
If I sleep alone forever she'll never come back.
Her cloakclasp shining in starlight at the edge of an ocean.
Her plaid flapping in the southern wind at the world's rim.

1986

HELLHOUND MEMOS

(1993)

for Terry Kelly and Nicholas Johnson

I got to keep movin'
 I got to keep movin'
  blues falling down like hail
U m m m m m m m m m m m
  blues falling down like hail
   blues falling down like hail
And the days keep on worrying me
    there's a hell hound on my trail
    hell hound on my trail
     hell hound on my trail

ROBERT JOHNSON

[1]

Sunk in my darkness at daylight.
Rain on lamb's oily wool
my anointment.
Sunk in my darkness in my cracked
braindrain.
Daydawn lies here spastic as anything.
Knockings, roarings, sounds arrive
from one more planet you have not been to.

Not one child leaps up to say bravo!

Sunk in my darkness, weeping in trimmed maythorn
by petrol stations. They want my discount, my
coupon crystal goblet.
My phlegm, your phlegm.

Weak-kneed sunk in my blueness, my sun
your sun. My fuck-up, your fuck-up.
My rain, your rain.

All aboard and welcome.

[2]

Sunk at my crossroads, hellhounds baying
broken from chains, lips, jaws
slavering with death notice, rape
on my left and right, filthy money, yellow Jerusalem.
I'd walk in there, turn the tables, rinse
the crowd with phlegm, make their shoes walk.
Swag wings at the con machines, blister
fingers of the three lemon fools. Sing mad,
merle mad, trill a bone, door stance finally
with contre-jour, say what next ammonite, how
is oxygenation, where's your Elvis lipcurl now?

[3]

Me the multiplex moron, multigenerational
multiplicity, many-fingered man with a violet
shell suit, stolen BMW and a rack of E. I'm here!

I used to be nowhere, now I'm all over the place.
I've had the garlic and thyme, the purging flax, blood and bone.
I've been to bed with the black pudding. Keep it.

I'm the only jackpot chancer on the job, estate joy-rider
extraordinaire. Bored in the listless
summer, when the boys in blue are in Marbella

I waft in or rev as is my nature, contrary to
council or ecclesiastical denial, and open up these
stolen microwaves. I turn them on and breathe.

I don't care what the damage is. Or the waste.
I enjoy the flames. I can scorch a line, a beautiful
blue and true line through the hull of your lives

and must say I like it better so. I adjust my visor
accordingly. Cut, cut, cut. It's my dark, dark memo,
almost a badge. I groove in the magenta heat, I lean

into it. I don't erect headstones, Hosanna those
sky-blue heavens in the fairy tales. I deliver.
Into a permanent darkness for the rest of your days.

I come down like slate-grey rain. That's all. No God available.

[4]

(for PBS one day early)

The very low odour tough acrylic formula
of B&Q Safe Paint with satin gloss finish
is venal. Civilisation too good a word for it.
Percy, why won't anyone leave us alone? Pass
The 10-litre can of Professional Obliterating Paint,
please. Pass the zinc-plated wing nuts, the spur
budget gold effect bracket and inspiration shelf.
Not to mention the Zamba Wall Shelving with Tool Rack
Hardbeam I am for both of us against the intrusions.
Bysshe, tush, fash not, two hundred is nothing.
Wait until two thousand, then we'll justly explode!
The very floodlit light of heaven has already been
sold, as you predicted. Nothing to attract you
but the chard and sprouting broccoli. The rest is trash.
Babble, babble, babble. Slick, stink, stink.
Happy birthday, wake up, let's drown together!

[8]

Now that the vast furtherance of widespread publicity
for the degree course in how to be a complete nobody
twice over if you're lucky has won a number of awards
it is altogether time to nip under the plover's wing
and sleep. It is time to hug the lamb and mushroom.
It is time to pluck the rosemary, the rue, the swaying dill.

O we will sleep and rest there. We shall be most quiet.
Lord I know ye will find me a place in a lonnen where
I can curl sockless, no matter where the sun is, beyond
any future scars, far from fire, far from phlegm and
any fame, please. So much I need darkness to surround my head.

Though I am bent, straighten me.

[9]

God bless you little girl the lean dry hand
wrote on her forehead as the knife went in.

[10]

> *Today we walk by love*
> BLISS CARMAN

Trouble on all sides today up and down:
Palms of my feet, soles of my hands.
No rain on lambs' wool, no anointment under the elder tree.
Wealth of sickness streaming.
Four fingers over my right eye, I don't want to see it.
But you con it with freak sight, provoked all my life,
eyes hammered by destruction winds.
Sunlit laurels I am not fit to wear
winking reflections like Aidan's fingernails.

Alone without lipstick she said in the lit doorway:
I cannot speak in cogent sentences but still you will not
                                                terrify me.
I have seen all of the films and you are not worse than them.
I have been to the top of the cairn for you, northern prince,
and I died every inch of the way.
I listened to the piper and it made me sick.

Nothing will bring me back: no herbal verbals, no award-winning
regional disease, coal mines for example.
No sex with wet hair. No gin and talc.
I'll just wash and go.

[11] *Linda Manning Is a Whore*

She moves in tumult.
ROBERT HUGHES BENSON

Wisdome flew upon me tonight like a bat's wing.
I was at Dunton roundabout
shaking hands with Robert Johnson and the Jesus Christ Almighty.
I could hear the elderberries crying dew.
I was going to ferment them into maniac milk.
Bubbles everywhere.
O my knees broke and I sank to my feet.
I ploated the stupid sky for even daring to wake up,
honked on the moon, slapped a pizza margherita
in the sun's face, saying: Quench in my hart the flames
of badd desyre so foolishly addressed.
Who can blot out the Crosse I heard her say.
Batter my eyelids, knock me down, I will be an usurpte towne
all by myself, betrothed to an enemie, made by men's hands
to kiss the lips of another: Some glue-sniffer sprawled
unconscious in Hood Street.

I am a woman, no chief dignitie for me.

[13] *Shaking Minds with Robespierre*

Levellers and prince-fingerers quartered in the heather.
Once I was an antirrhinum with a hot dry position.
Now I'm disposable with a seedbed of debatable facts.
I can hear the hellhounds carping and crapping
all over the cairn and the law. Suddenly
one will flame out
from shook foil to fang a breast.

I ruck
and roll the house
but that snot-streaming bitch
rides my well-punched eyelids up and down
and fills my spleen with gall.
I miss my stew-bearing Mary,
cusloppe stains upon her hand-made hem.

O to be a snowflake, whipped in by easterlies,
soaking gardens and allotments until the lupin and peony seeds
descend;
I want to be bright shining
as cuticles in the Dunton nursery.
Bright as Aidan's eyes.

Yet once more I am taxed
as hounds paw leek flags and onion beds,
scarring the enriched loam, eager to run.

Tonight we try Sarah Ferguson.
I must collect my papers and go.

[18] *Wringing the Shingle*

I'll be down at the dock in the morning.
The brisk cutlets of the breakers
flash contrast to the sky.
Foam wringing the shingle is from the strange mouth
of Anne Sexton.
She was at the bayside chemist last night.
Robert's long gone, up at three, leaving his queen of spades,
down the highway to the next county fair.
There's a glass of poisoned whiskey waiting for him
and it won't be from a white man's hand.
The ambulance will be slow.
He'll be plain stiff chocolate toes turned up on the slab
just like Bessie.

Pinned again to the wire, eyes clammed.
Raven hair blown and burned. Charred to the follicle.
Wristblood glued to the Nazi connection.
Zip done up.
Laughter lasting as long as she loved him.
She walked Poland with ten league eyes.

Sexton toppled in tonight
crashing into the doctor's blue swivel chair.
We fed her stomach to the drain
and walked her home.

[19]

The darkness fell, and all the glory vanished.
AUGUSTA THEODOSIA DRANE

Vapour rises from the ducts and flues, ashen and feathered
against the Batman cape sky like smoked bone, ascending
wounded inside the theoretical bruising, burdened
with the small matter of mankind and the grit
in its windows and eyes, which are silver and aquamarine
here in the Fauvist metropolis.

The world with hate and envy raging
surveys its wild forsaken hoots, and the lanceolate leaves, still
fragrant, ready for the pan, are quivering under the fjord blasts tonight.
Sleet penetrates the weave.
Chapped fingers play the bottleneck
at Gallowgate crossroads
where we have lost Robert Johnson to some deep connection
down the hellhound trail
passing Anne Sexton details of the Christmas late chemist rota.
Beneath the blue star are bilious pools of maniac milk.
Yet once more we enter the falsedom in scarlet and gold,
attracted by automatic defrost function
and full range of hostess trollies available.

Snow blurs the moon
and the sky is whipped by the blizzard's tail.
it is all like smoke
in the swiftly changing heads of the trees.

PEARL

(1995/1997)

for Jackie

Looking Down From The West Window

I smashed my wings
against the rain-soaked deck
and was happy you lifted me
into your safe fingers and palms.
If not too disgusted, hold me
close forever keenly.

Sweet Jesus: Pearl's Prayer

Listen, hark, attend; wait a moment
as they used to say
in the ancient tongue of literacy, before
language was poisoned to a wreckage, which
you will find for a fee (going up)
in your earpiece, inside
the wainscoted foyer
of the Museum of Stupidity down in the dumps:
Permit me to say this on a grey roofslate, as I protect
my poor writing, I can't do joined up, with soaked forearm
from the driving rain – I am Pearl.
Please estrange your children, and your bairns' bairns
from terrible tabloidations, scored into
your blood in the sorriest ink.
O paranoid Marxist Cambridge prefects,
self-appointed guarantors of consonants and vowels
and arrangement of everyday sentences, placing
of punctuation marks, with which Pearl
wished to be in steady flux, she said
with fingers, eyes, thumbs and palms. Listen.

When the borage flowers closed at night
she moved against me, rain lashed facing
west to the law, whispering: There is so much
wickedness.
They want to tax my ABC, they want to jail my tongue.
I dream their high-up heather deaths
though I do not emit articulate sound.
I am just a common white swan.
Fierce I am when I want, want
my milky hands on my destroyers, rive
them apart like a marauding riever, or
down south, roll you in the Nene, without
Dunlop lace-up boots, one bare foot
should do it, spate or trickle you'll be face down.
Spade job later, midnight special, I've got
one somewhere, I know mam has; bury
you all deep, lead tunnels or out on the Fens.

I cannot cease to dream and speak of Pearl.

Pearl's Utter Brilliance

Argent moon with bruised shawl
discreetly shines upon my frozen tongue tonight
and I am grinning handclap glad.
We loved so much the lunar light
on rawbone law or splashing in the marigold beds,
our gazing faces broken in the stream.
Taut, not taught, being kept from school
was a disgrace, single word 'idiot' chalked
on the yard wall: soaked in sleet, sliding
in snow beneath a raft of sighs, waiting
for the roar of an engine revved before
daybreak, as the world, the permanent wound
I would never know in sentence construction, fled
away from my heather-crashing feet, splash happy
kneefalls along the tumblestones,
whip-winged plovers shattering the dew.
Each day up here I am fiercely addressed
by the tips of the trees; said all I could
while heifers moaned in the stalls, clopping
of hooves my steaming, shitting
beast accompaniment. And these giant clouds.
Pity? Put it in the slurry with the rest of your woes.
I am Pearl, queen of the dale.

Pearl Says

Down from the rain-soaked law
and the rim of the world
where even on misty nights
I can see the little lights
of Penrith and Kendal and, yes,
Appleby, and hear the clatter of unshoed
horses which pound like my heart,
I also sense the moss greened underwater
stones of the Eden to the west. I trim
the wick for mam's asleep now, dad
long gone to Cumberland and work, and
read read my exercise books filled
with stories by Bar, my trout-catching
hero, dragons and space ships, sketches
in crayons you can't buy anymore.
When I stand on the top road and bow
in sleet, knuckle-bunching cold, or
slide over dead nettles on snow, do
not mistake my flung out silhouetted
limbs for distant arches and viaducts.
I am not bringing you legendary feats
of sophisticated engineering. I in
worry eat my fist, soak my sandwich
in saliva, chew my lip a thousand times
without any bought impediment. Please
believe me when my mind says and
my eyes send telegraphs: I am Pearl.
So low a nobody I am beneath the cowslip's
shadow, next to the heifers' hooves.
I have a roof over my head, but none
in my mouth. All my words are homeless.

No Such Thing

Grassblade glintstreak in one of the last mornings
before I come to meet you, Pearl,
as the rain shies. How bright and sudden the dogrose,
briefly touched by dew, flaming
between the deep emerald and smoky blue.
Dogrose, pink as Pearl's lips, no
lipstick required, what's that mam, no
city chemist or salon. We set
our colour charts in the rain
by feldspar heaved from the streambed;
cusloppe, burn peat in summer
and wild trampled marigolds.
Pearl, somewhere there is a stern receiver
and all accounts are open in the rain.
Once more through the heifer muck
and into the brilliant cooling of the watermint beds.
Sky to the west today, where you are, Pearl, is
a fantastic freak bruise which hurts the world.
Coward rain scared of our joy refuses to come.
Deep despair destroys and dents delight
now that I have pledged my future to you, Pearl,
from the edge of the roaring bypass, from
the home of the broken bottle and fiery
battleground of the sieged estate.

Mony Ryal Ray

For urthely herte myght not suffyse
— PERLE

Skybrightness drove me
to the cool of the lake
to muscle the wind
and wrestle the clouds
and forever dream of Pearl.
O Pearl, to speak in sentences, using
all the best vowels and consonants, is argent sure.
Smoke drifts over slow as Pearl's fingers
fanning through the borage groves
and the world vigorous again
in pursuit of renewal.
Pearl into Hexham
with cleft palate: the market, into Robbs
for curtains believe it or not, orders
written out by mam to be handed over, post
office adjacent to the war memorial,
bus station.
Billy driving Pearl home on the Allenheads bus, off
here, pet?, and round
the turning circle
by the heritage centre
to be opened by an adulterous prince.
Pearl saying when asked by a dale stranger,
'Where's the way to The Grapes?':
a-a-a-a-a-a-a-.

Only the magnificent peewit more eloquent than Pearl.

No Buses To Damascus

Wonder Pearl distemper pale, queen
of Blanchland who rode mare Bonny
by stooks and stiles in the land
of waving wings and borage blue
and striving storms of stalks and stems.
Pearl, who could not speak, eventually
wrote: Your family feuds are ludicrous.
Only my eyes can laugh at you.
She handed over springwater under a stern look.
We fell asleep at Blackbird Ford
named by princes Bar and Paul of Sparty Lea.
We splashed and swam and made the brown trout mad.
Dawdled in our never-ending pleasure over
earth-enfolded sheephorns
by rivermist webs, half-hidden moss crowns.

Up a height or down the dale in mist or shine
in heather or heifer-trampled marigold
the curlew-broken silence sang its volumes.
Leaning on the lichen on the Leadgate Road,
Pearl said: a-a-a-a-a-, pointing with perfectly poised
index finger towards the rusty coloured dry stone wall
which contrasted so strongly with her milky skin.

The congenital fissure in the roof of her mouth
laid down with priceless gems, beaten lustrous copper
and barely hidden seams of gold.

Pearl Suddenly Awake

Banged my right hand
against the chipped middle drawer
in the corner of the west-facing bedroom, sucking
home the knuckle blood.
Once more I rose
and kneeled, praying to God, and rose again,
my tongue in everlasting chains.
Bless him asleep with his yellow hair,
worn out with wandering, map-reading
the laws and lanes and trails.
Cowslips, our rushing ancient stream,
years of rain sweeping over the cairns,
beautifully soft, distinctly-shaped moss and lichen
enfolding the retrieved tumblestones,
steps to our great and mad adventures.
We laughed off cuts and bruises falling in the tadpole pools.
In my mind at the top of the valley,
roar of lead ore poured crashing
into the ghosts of now forsaken four-wheeled bogies
distinctly off the rails. They –
you call it government – are killing everything
now. Hard hats abandoned in heather. Locked-up
company huts
useless to bird, beast or humankind. Tags
in the rims: Ridley, Marshall,
McKinnon and Smith. Deserted
disconnected telephones, codes
and names I could not read.
Dead wires
left harping in the high wind
that always sang to me.
Day dawn dripping of dew
from those greenly dark feathers of fern, beneath
fragrant needles of fir and pine
as the stars swing into place
above our double gaze at heaven.

Fever

Pearl, I'm singing Fever to you
but still in the bland auditorium the stupid voices explode.
No one but you is listening.
We are back in the sheepfield chasing a rabbit again.
The rain is from the dark west tonight, raced along
by the sharply pushed-out breath of Pearl.
She has tramped with her cleft to the law, soaked cairn,
OS number recorded once for future use
but forgotten in the slap of heifer rumps.
In her little-fingered grip of the full-buttoned coat,
hair maddened by such a storm, lips pursed; my heroine, not
bothered with Kendal Mintcake, tugger of shirts and cuffs and hair.
She opens her swan mouth and rain pours in from north
and south and west, Atlantic squalls from Donegal.
They cannot lubricate her speech.
A baked canyon there, my Pearl.
At 3 I woke, rolled and twisted all my milky wrists
around the iron bedposts, heart ransomed to Pearl, her
Woolworth butterfly blue plastic clip, still made in Britain
then, her flighty bow.
Due east she looks, lashed by rain one side, yonder
just mist wet, heather splashes in the gale, towards the broken
ovens of manufacture and employment, and to the new units
in green and red, with almost literate noticeboards,
development corporation
fast-growing shrubs (emerald tops and silver undersides:
pound notes with roots), not with
the tramp, tramp, tramp
of men and women going home.
Transport of the rain where Pearl is, is
taken care of forever,
long after we have gone, into the cracked peat
we have not cut, taken to the channels,
onto becks and springs, to the borage groves
and streaming watermint.
At 4 I woke again
with torment, unpunished badness and unjudged blame.
That night, Pearl faced the lightning alone.
She could not even speak to encourage her own bravery.
Last seen by me tongue far out as it would go
just acting like a gutter or a gargoyle
praying for St Elmo's fire up here on the Cushat Law
to surge her diction down the alphabet trail.

The Shells Her Auburn Hair Did Show

(for Stephen Bierley)

Good morning Pearl, good morning John,
good morning the Jesus Christ Almighty;
good morning Stephen, transferring
to the Alps from Lac de Madine:
I know your heart's in Helpston today.
Pearl walked barefoot down the rain-soaked flags last night, fearful
of smoke and fire, with words on the slate: Where do I go
to bang MY head? Where will I find a workshop
sustained by Strasbourg grants
and European funny money, with instruments
modern enough to replace the canyon in the roof of my mouth?
Government? What does that mean?
Stephen, best friend of Barry, travelling in France, father
of Rachel and Timothy, husband of Sarah, what
does a government do? Can it make you speak?
I leak truth like a wound, sore not seen to.
Call me a scab if you wish, I'm still plain Pearl.
Wild Knitting was named after me, I know you did, Bar.
Every day – I wake at four – tongue fever grasps me
and I am possessed: though
my screen is blank and charmless to the human core
I have an unbending desire to marry consonants and vowels
and mate them together
in what you call phrases and sentences
which can become – imagine it – books!
I'd like to sit down with Stephen, inside the borage groves, sing him
my songs of the stream.
But of course I cannot.
My cuticles above singular fields
of harvested grain, when torched stubble is nowhere
near the heat of the burning grief
in my illiterate heart, when I can only hope to extinguish it
with unfettered tears, at four in the morning, when no one else
is awake.
I walk to the wetted garden where the lawn is short.
All the skies are leased anyway. Nothing is owned
by humans. It is an illusion nightmare.
You fall through the universe
clinging to unravelled knots and breaking strings.
John eating grass. Percy drinking brine.
No B&Q in my day. No proper ABC.
My mouth a wind-tunnel. I flew like a moth in its blast.
Take my hand and put me right.
This is the end of the bulletin from the end of the road.

Pearl Alone

Yes, I am not emitting articulate sound.
I take my stand and – deliberately – refuse to plead.
There is no adoration in my mute appeal.
My tongue a pad or cone for the trumpet's bell.
Tongue-tied, bereft of ABC, I lap
and soak my whistle at the law's rim.
In mood moments
I say smash down the chalkboard:
let it stay black.
Shake my chained tongue, I'll fake a growl – a-a-a-a-a-.
Dog my steps, I am wet-toed to the spring
for mam's tea: spam on Sundays
and chips if there is coal.
In the Orient I would be a good servant
willing to please.
Damping of strings my speciality,
an hired mourner
for the rest of my days: gazer
at umbrellas and rain.
No use for owt else up here
except wiping my legs of heifer muck
and fetching the four o'clock milk.
In the byre alone I weep
at the imagined contrivance
of straps and wires
locking my loll-tongue gargoyle head.
My muzzle gushes rain
and I wince when people speak to mam,
giving me their sideways look.
My eyes go furious and I stamp, stamp, stamp.
Pulse fever even in Hartfell sleet.
Loud tumult, what there is of my mind
tumbled into the lashing trees. Yes,
I love falling, caught momentarily
through each tall command of branches, amazed once more
at the borage blue sky
in another September afternoon
with tongue spouting, soaking the cones, thudding
to the very ground, disturbing
all the birds and worms and wasps and bees.
Don't count on me for fun
among the towering cowslips,
but please don't crush my heart.

Cavalry At Calvary

(for Maggie O'Kane)

All aboard, it's party time, with
my averring slut receptionist.
In the land of panty punishment,
she's king.
I traipsed around in belting sleet
the glades and glens
searching my ghost of Pearl.
Pearl in borage by the tadpole pool.
Pearl on the law, hair lashed backward,
facing the great west wind
from Alston and Nenthead.
Pearl on Noble's trailer, squinting into the sun,
lambing done for the day.
Then I lost my mind in Sarajevo: twice, every night.
I was all hitched up with a dying beauty, Irma Hadzimuratovic,
across four columns, 12 cems deep, final edition. She was stable
at the time
but I could not stop dreaming of Pearl,
her bare feet driving the brown trout mad.
We were Herculesed out of Sarajevo, terrifically
muscular, Spielberg almost, and
everyone spoke of us in harried whispers,
7, 9, or 10 o'clock tones, we were moved around
like pit pony adverts, double column change please, page nine.
Panic over, the doctor said.
Irma, I know the surgeons have rebuilt your bowels and your back.
Irma, in the agony of the night, in the filthy bombshell bombhell,
under the nostrils of the TV cameras, freak show
brilliance, foaming at the mouth
for the worldwide page of the *Shields Gazette*, baby. Irma,
dying on your little side, arm the colour of fresh milk.
Irma, page one if there's nowt better, pet,
for this edition only,
I love you today as much as Pearl.

From The Land Of Tumblestones

O the rare gold
under the tips of the trees.
October the long shadows, new jobs with the power station
over the law, strange restlessness of winter, ovens
long closed down the dale.
The cold-blooded couriers of planned unemployment
were not then in full station.
Again I woke at four, sky tar-black, then the bull
over Africa, and heard him go, quarter-ironed,
thunder-heeled to the west, to Penrith and Appleby, Olympia
hammering out chrysanthemum and leek show results.
Long time over the law he was back, longing
for my saliva-gushing tongue, my path spittle,
my bright-eyed, brown-eyed face, my grip fingers
when berry collecting, red or blue, in our
upland empire.
I moved my hands in little mitts as best I could.
We strode together daily
over sullen ghosts of lead,
the boom of collapsed shafts,
no longer mastered by men. Cold ovens.
Borage groves sawn down by Jack
in the night.
Eventually I would write, not say,
I loved you, special consonants and vowels
recorded on paper up here
in the high country: white water,
foaming tumblestones, wet and grey days, or
brilliant Aprils and Septembers, shine, shine, shine,
I loved you absolutely all of the time.

Dark Was The Night And Cold Was The Ground

Pearl: beautiful lustre, highly prized gem,
precious one, finest example of its kind,
dewdrop, tear of Mary, reduced by attrition
to small-rounded grains.
Pearl in the Borage up to her waist.
Pearl in the wildmint.
Pearl in the wind-spilled water.
Pearl flecked in the sunlight, one
foot here, one there, knuckles on hips
on the stile, all angles and charms.
Pearl adrift in the rain through the whispering burn.
So much sighing at her own distress: a-a-a-a-a-a-.
Pearl looks in the mirror of the molten water,
sticks out her tongue and all you get
is a splash on the path.
I looked into her face and was humbled once again.
Lipstick, she said, on a slate in the rain,
is a complete nobody to me.
I'd like a square meal daily
for me and my mam.

Pearl And Barry Pick Rosehips For The Good Of The Country

Hammers and pinions, sockets, fatal faces
and broken bones. That was after Pearl.
All mornings the sapphire sky, judge wig clouds, here
to Dunbar, made especially gentle because
turned left towards Ireland and soft rain, air delicious
with scent of borage and thyme, dreaming, dreaming,
dreaming and dreaming of Pearl. She gripped her Co-op coat
and she gripped me, bonds not lost in azure eternity.
When yearning for correct connections
of consonants and vowels, verbal vagaries not excluded,
taking into addition
my often gobsmacked face, when I did not tug
fast enough pointing to the dipper's nest.
We went to pick rosehips in the upland raw, above
the whitewater and the falling tumblestones.
Blue days raced by like a Hexham builder's van
late for lunch. We crushed a heady brew
of grass and fern, and loved the slate grey rain.

Surge, surge, I feel today, in the law drizzle, after
tugging my Bar, but my tongue won't move.
I am just a strange beak, purring with my fruit.
Open my mouth and water fountains down.
I am responsible for the pool on the path.

She had the most amazing eyes in history.

Those Sandmartin Tails

(for Holly Hunter)

I could never speak.
What good was I to anyone?
I have, I learned later, the emotions
of literate people: joyed when it shined, sun
so fierce in the molten white water it took my breath away.
I washed my hair beneath the ice-cold tumblestones.
At night the wide-awake dream – waterproof
lace-up Dunlop boots.
We stretched our limbs in sheets of rain
on the Killhope or Cushat, thumbing and fingering
rain off our west-facing faces.
Donegal sleet spoke to our faces uniquely,
eyes a furnace of hazel and blue.
Pearl I was and am, standing alone
in the October spokeshadows of the hospital trees.
Pearl I was and am, firm fingered with nails
well cut, red mittens and bright smiles, alone
in the streambed, feldspar and quartz, no words available.
Deftly-ladled ankles, thanks to God, opal
in the law light, toes wetted in the berylmintbed.
Frost on the earth stiffens my clicking backdoor tongue,
and despite the joy of a surging stream
it is late and my soul is dark.

Woe, Woe, Woe

(for Jim Greenhalf)

All of you with consonants and vowels
and particular arrangement of phrases and sentences
spoken and written, should have seen my eyebrows
move around, my hands and arms go crazy.
Not least you saw me lick the drizzle
from the aching door post I leaned against,
thinking it would lubricate my poorly-engineered tongue.
Many of you shied away
but it was really me who had the hurt
as the argent rising moon looked in.
I had a little Woolworth blackboard
and the heathens want to tax my ABC.
I move my outstretched fingers gently, natural
in a long-grassed, wind-moved world
under this cobalt sky: O what delight
to hear the dippers up the road
drinking in an April morning.
Yes, yes, it is true: I am always worried,
fretting by the gate at the turn in the lane.
All of that law rain soaking my face
upturned to heaven. Once more a prayer unsaid.
I can be fierce nonetheless
to help hug against the many sores.
Hands, palms, right and left, hardened
by bucket-filling, bucket-fetching,
bringing spring water for mam, slopping out beast clarts.
Sick of it sometimes in the hard dark mornings
and unable to adequately say so
I throw the pails helter-skelter into the stinking drain hole,
smiling quietly for you only.

Blizzard: So Much Bad Fortune

(for Jackie Litherland)

I tear apart the smart brochures
in my fit, my ABC war.
Wind heaving tonight in the red berries and branches.
Lit windows suddenly revealed in their stone shoulders.
Halt I am with alphabet arrest, up
a height in the snow my croaking throat soaked.
Argent water hurled against the shifting tumblestones.
Fierce bidding for space between me and the gale.
Idiot, the wall said. Person so deficient in mind
as to be permanently incapable of rational conduct;
colloquial: stupid person.
My tongue abandoned with unmade key.
In my brain a terrible country, violent and wild.
All those unspaced paving stones,
all those untravelled distances,
all of those sentences frozen in time.
I can say less than a dog.
Hailstones from Ireland and America thrown in my face,
a duly convicted human full stop.
In fragrant marigold heaven
then I am not so fierce, so tongue-blind, dreaming
of telling dales tales to who will listen,
hands in the borage, toes in the watermint.
The curlew's cry my daily ode to beauty and delight.
Is not the peewit's high-up heather song all poetry to me?

Lost Pearl

My hands are in the clouds again, thumping the sun.
And then I would be a wild, not mild, child,
stamping my feet and cry, cry, cry,
looking up at the mesmeric flicker of adult mouths
as they said A and E and I and U and O, all joined up
in terrible tresses, looking down at me,
not quite forgiving mam my swollen grave inconsequence.
I held myself in a corner laughing
when they moved around their pretty vowels and consonants.
Outside, are they blisters of hurt on the moon?
Or the rims of craters before you fall defeated
with the dogs on your blood?
Will I return forty years from now – 1998 –
to find the chalkboard frozen, nibs
broken, inkwell shards scattered to four walls
by Irish gales, through shattered windows, and
no one ready to pick up a pen to say this:
sentences are not for prisoners only.
Now I will circle and uncircle
my index fingers forever alone
in the pools, spelling and unspelling
our tragic consequences, smiling
then not smiling, sunshine on
borage and the restless waves of bees,
rain and the silenced creak of the
stile gate, because of the mixture
of oil, dripped in the hinges
from the emerald painted neck
of the spoon-armed, thin nozzled
drip-drop oil can – Castrol – and, yes, my dear,
thank you for helping me over.
We walked there and nearby always so very kindly.

Pearl's Poem Of Joy And Treasure

Spout, pout, spout. Put my spittle all about.
Bare feet pressing down wet upon the glamorous
deciduous rugs of gold. Otherwise
needles and cones, sheep bones, crisps
and ox-cheek for tea.
Dark despair around benights me.
Above the burn I listen for the turn
of the water over tumblestones,
wag my tongue like a wand
in the law wind. Fierce light
invades my eyes and shut face, closed for the night.
Unable to sleep, despite the hardness of the day,
I cluck and purr.
Why am I ashamed of my permanent silence?
In the brilliant heather, shin deep, I am
a good lass, purring and foaming, friend of green breasted
plover, keen listener to the wind in the wires; all
the bees and beasts understand
my milky fingers and palms.
I whet my whistle in the same pools –
at one with the world.
This white water upland empire, hidden
moss grows in the cracks.
I felt my way there when climbing
the bank, press my head there, soft emerald cushions,
when summer sleep takes on.
The wind runs and roars from the west, from the ferry landings
of Ireland; I listen for the freshly falling tumblestones,
long and long until tears almost drown me
for consonants and vowels, sentences of good measure,
for an understanding of the very word syntax, brought
to my cavernous mouth, practising the words Appleby, Penrith, Shap.
Rosehip plucker, mitts needing repair,
here mam, on the sideboard, longing
for the words capital letter, Ordnance Survey map, to
read the true height of the law, emphasise my longing.
Twine my tongue and ease its itch.
Make the sky so borage blue.
Let the argent stars shine upon my upturned smiling face
and furnish me with hope.
I need all the love I can hold.

Pearl At 4 a.m.

Moon afloat, drunken opal shuggy boat
in an ocean of planets and stars.
Fierce clouds gather over me
like a plaid shawl.
Gone, gone, click of quarter irons
to Nenthead, Alston and beyond.
I moved my mouth in the darkness of the kitchen,
spittle poured wrongfully into the pan fat.
Snow once more
in my broken face, reduced
to licking the swollen door post. Just a gargoyle.
Death upon us like a stalking foot-soldier, high
and mighty on the law, bayonet
fixed. A sudden glint there, and that's it.
Spluttering lard
and strange sparks
ignite my mind, for I am in love
with something I do not know.
It is the brusque wind,
the nearest falling tumblestones
dislodged by the spate, the finest
snowdrops under heaven.

Pearl's Final Say-So

Fusillade of the sun's eye-piercing darts.
Then sky from Dunbar and the long curve strands
arrives laden with rain: O these winds which move
my golden hair and heart and the fierce tips
of my beloved whispering trees.
The damage has been done with moon-kissed me, running
and racing downhill, flung beside myself
with silence or groans into clart-filled ditches and drains.
Where is my fierce-eyed word warrior today? Slap with violence
all you wish night and day, my language Lancelot – left hand
margin Olympia 5022813 – ABC impossible – and
I struggle and struggle but mean to win my way in
(cat, sat, bat, mat!): only the peewit,
the puffed lark – look at him rise ardent-breasted
as the tractor comes by – and chough with poetry
in the grass-turning, wind-burning morning. Say Nowt.
Sun and rain, wild perfume in my poor clothes
from heather and bilberry and the faint remaining
smell of sheep-dip on my neatly-sewn hem by mam, all wild
as anything on the Cushat. Then as the great winds sweep
across my frozen tongue I lean and lie and weep
for want of proper placing of full stops and all other means
of regular punctuation; I draw them in the grass
but the wind just drives them away from me. Wet-footed
I tread home alone as the beasts are put in and the byres closed.
Lance, lance, Lancelot, let me practise that, index fingers
working the keys, corporal acting as sergeant: yes, leave
your argent blade inside my aching brain, its light
will help me find the way towards the proper letters of my ABC –
for I am Pearl, idiot by ford and stile, stile which does
not squeak now, idiot awash beneath the tumblestones,
receiver and glad conjuror of hailstones from the law
whose inevitable forwarding address is my face and knuckles
and who will forever be the agents which cool my blood.
And mam has let the stove die – not like her – so it is cold tonight.
Typewriter he taught me down the dale – mitts on – Red mittens –
and the sun's last lances lingering lovingly in Penrith
& Kirkby Stephen, where clatter of brief-legged ponies
hammered in my heart, but mossbank stones pillowed my spirit:
before the awesome black velvet went over my eyes
up a height in the last wilderness on the frozen law.
Those faraway jewels and halo brooches rived from darkness:
Stars!

THE BOOK OF DEMONS

(1997)

for Jackie Litherland
beloved comrade and warrior queen

Ode To Beauty Strength And Joy And In Memory Of The Demons
(for Jackie Litherland)

1

Forgive me for my almost unforgivable delay – I have been laying the world
to waste
beyond any faintest signal of former recognition. For a start, a very
brief beginning
on my relentless destruction trail, I made the dole queues longer for they did not
circle the earth in the dire band of misery I had wished and hoped
before my
rise to power among the global demons.
All my demons, my demonic hordes, reborn Stasi KGB neck-twisters
and finger crushers, their overcoats the width of castles
fashioned from the skins of Jews and poets, rustle with a fearful symphony
within the plate-sized buttons, rustling pipistrelles
and other lampshade bats. Some carry zipper body bags,
black and gleaming in the acid rain, from the mouths of others
words in Cyrillic Venusian torture chamber argot
stream upwards red on banners backwards
in a pullet neck-breaking snap in the final perversion
of the greatest revolutionary poster that
ever lived: the Suprematist Heart.
And don't forget, he will not let you forget, the man with the final
beckon, the forefinger locked in deadly
fearful invite. This demon, this gem-hard
hearted agent of my worst nightmare, this MC with spuriously
disguised gesture, this orchestrator of ultimate hatred,
the man with no eyes, no cranium, no brow no hair.
He will always be known as the Demon with the Mouth of Rustling
Knives, and the meshing and unmeshing blades
are right in your face. The blades say: there are your
bags. Pack them and come with us. Bring your bottles
and leave her. The contract is: you drink, we don't. The
rustling bats stay sober. When drunk enough they gather on your face
and you stand upon the parapet. You sway here and she is utterly
forgotten.
All that matters are the sober bats and the lampshade overcoats, which
press towards the edge above the swollen tide. You jump, weighed with
empty bottles in a number of bags – some hidden as it happens of which
you were ashamed inside your stupid sobering torment. And of course
we jump, arms all linked, with you into the fatal tidal reach. We also
pay a price. But the demon who shall always be known as the Mouth
of Rustling and Restless Knives, he stands upon the parapet. Never dies.
And all that can be heard beyond the wind are the relentless blades.

2

And then there is the pure transmission of kissing you, when
solar winds seethe in amber wonder through the most invisible wisps
   and strands in a tender half-lit prairie sometimes, caught in
light which is not quite light, but as if the entire world was drenched slate,
   or reflected thereof, in the soon to be handsome dawn of a reckless
damp November, with the gunmetal heavens plated quite beautifully
   in goldleaf of fallen nature already so readily ready for the rising
sap of a dearest darling spring when we will start again and the curtains
   will not be drawn at dawn beneath the monumental viaduct of the
great engineer. The truly great span of the legs above the city, spread
   and wide, rodded north and south and electrified by power passing
through beneath the novas and planets and starres. Magnetised!

Free Pet With Every Cage

Get out the shotgun put it in the gunrack.
Here I am gargoyled and gargled out,
foam then blood,
Flatface to Nilsville. In the toe-tag toerag dark,
siege upon his paling, wires berserk like cyborg fingers
in the demon neon's placid acid rain.
All the faery cars are shattered, overparked.
This is the hell time of the final testament,
the ultimate booking, the whipped out ticket, little Hitler
with Spitfire pencil on permanent jack-up; when he's not red
carding
your fanned-out fucked-up Bournville chocolate cheekbones
he's planning an invasion down your throat.
Big Jack with the bad crack,
just so peak and gleaming visor, ferret eyes
glinty like fresh poured Tizer – the seepage of the coleslaw,
the duff mayonnaise.
This is the season of firestorm lightning, torment time
of hell is beautiful.
Wide-awake hell, hell with fingers in a tightened vice,
forget the armies of little white mice,
hell beribboned with garotted larks and lice.
Yes, hell is beautiful, the weirdest ABC ever spoken
here in the dead letter box
in Crap Future Lane.
Wind clicks the metal leaves tonight.
I speed alive in sequence deep,
beast field rain
throbbing to the lipless pulse of windwonder.
O tormented landscape, handscape,
deathbones hewed
at my pouldrons and gorgets. Down
in the tarred and feathered department
of gutted souls the cry is so wimp: What's in it for me
but the Labour Party and geometric raisin bread?
Chomp, chomp, go the pink bleat sheep,
down to Walworth Road.
I'm such a bad and drunken lad, a fiend fellow
in the useless art of swallowing and wallowing,
as to invite brazenly her puckerage, her mayoral
addresses of correction, her buzzing network
of helplines flashing down the gorge.

Just look, I snarled my lute
in waspish worsement, claggy gob
clipped claptight shut.
I sledged it fast off my funny bondage tongue
but no one believed me above the cellar: I died
every day since I gave up poetry
and swapped it for a lake from the châteaux of France
and all of the saints – Bede, Bob, Sexton, Messrs Rotten, Johnson,
Presley and Cash – abandoned me.

Perhaps the purple plush pansies have an answer today.
Only my little yellow lanterns
spring vinelike
in their breezy Jerusalem
aiming for victory over the ordinary sunne.

Hell is the pavement against my shit face.
And the devil has seen Robert off on the bus.
The light of recovery is just a format.
The light of recovery is just a lost fairy tale
seeping with ferndamp
in the bluebell vales of your childhood.
The light of recovery is an ex-starre, furious with everlasting
darkness.

I am the addict, strapping on his monumental thirst.
The sky is livid like jigsawed lace
and there are no happy endings.

Buying Christmas Wrapping Paper On January 12

Let loose at morning from frost pockets the wind rips.
Enough to snuff blue candles in a huff of sighs.
Let's use the sensational strong stuff hanging off the wall
before we electrocute ourselves forever
to a final gleam of love. We do it like a Miró or galvanised Matisse.
Her name is Bijou, her sign The Snake.
Three-storey monsters, whipcord Judas-faced accusers and sneaks, faking
that the very sky is human
filled with sham planets, nooses not yet minted
from lunar shards
at every broken tearful opportunity
while in retarded zones
the tumblestone temple tables are turned.
Heaven's just an opened bottle
                              in a demon's argent mitts
smuggled to my unholy lips
from the squirrelled reservoir, the cached stash
in Stasi lock-ups
underneath the fallen arches
in Legless Lonnen
                down Do-lalley Drive, Kerbcrawl Boulevard, Cirrhosis Street
and Wrecked Head Road:
I am leader of the beguiled and fear of straps across my chest
cleave me to the haunted floorboard bed.
Ruthless vanity will have its day (as you know worshipped ones)
and the Stasi demons' gin-soaked bat-packed overcoats
are not different, my grave advocates, my angels, allies, brave backers and boosters,
my eternal love donors,
my decency guarantors, armpit clutch helpers
jostling to seize me in my seizures
from the cobbled gutter's facedown drenched hell,
you patrons and dauntless promoters, partners and pals,
such confrères of confidence,
my duplicate equals and ferocious friends.

Vintage and grizzled each Satan's wretch
does purl, ooze, gurgle, spurt and twirl, gyrate,
pirouette, spin, reel and swim
in grim lashing bind, unswayable elbow grease
applied to mindcrazy moonshine not hindered.
Living daily rim to mouth, rev gun throttled, quelled and jammed,
too late to stop now.

Let the dead man walk to rise is sombre fiction
my murderers will never calibrate.
                              It and they are all upon me now
and tenebrous squalid and ignoble night
snaps its willing neck
on every lurid aspect of my rotten scowling face.

We Offer You One Third Off Plenitude

O let me plunge my feverhands into his clotted throat. Let me free
the devil's briars and combinations, even down upon my worn-out
woman's honkers, fingers hinged to wrench out infection
before it has him in the demon yard, the bad god shed, orangebox
overcoat so thinly laid.

There is more to his royal light than
wings of demon pipistrelles can dim, or dreaded Stasi hats and coats
undone to hide the starres and moon.
Busy to the last
with basin of detox vomit, I am black flag nurse, noose loosener,
penitence ring wrecker, rupture lip annihilator extraordinaire,
fierce defendress of flame faith, laver
of eclipsed kiss champ.

Revivor of the passed out poet in his pissed up plan.
In fit wrath, Notre Dame gutterspouts spring up
inside his fried lamb's liver face.

I am the woman accused: vulturefemme
pecking, beak brushing
Prometheus poisoned meat.
I am the woman admonished
with fitwords, spit bubbles
and green bad movie slime.

Yet wipe I do
to lie against him sober
when the fit has gone
and each defashioned jigsaw piece
back in place.
Yes, it is true, Albion is distressed upon her hardened knees.
The quality of mercy writ so large
upon his broken angelface.

So many darts
and drunken hurts and harms.
So many ill-formed hurtwords.
Such forays of spitting spouting guntongue.
Twelve per cent non-vintage gargoyle gurgle gobshite.

The 999 call – again.

My quivering man laid under a blue light
empty bottles left behind.

Daddy Wants To Murder Me

I write poetry at the age of seven and daddy wants to murder me.
He does a good imitation of it: beats me with a leather belt
and tears my little book in strips.
I wonder why my little poetry book, which is blue, is in strips,
and falling to the carpet like rain.
Strips and stripes, my daddy. An awesome man.
I sit in the garden reading Homer, shy lad
under a folding one-man tent and daddy wants to murder me.
Daddy, I caught a trout. Honest I did dad.
Daddy, I caught a dace away on holiday in Dorset
and it was argent like the moon when I ran, ran, I ran away
for fear of everything and you. It was argent like the moon.
It was argent daddy, but daddy wants to murder me.
Daddy, the wind murmurs and hoys against my shins
and I am alone upon my little pins in dales and hills
but my heart is chill: because daddy wants to murder me.
Daddy, do you want me to stop using the word daddy
and not write like Sylvia Plath at all?
Do you want me to write about my shrub of bay
which we can stroke on our way
out to the bender to have a hoolie and a ball? Do you daddy?
Normally, in recent literary history, daddy, it is women
who write about their daddies, daddy. But now it's me.
Daddy, da, pa, everytime I hear your name I want to flee, flee, flee.
Daddy, when the word *failure* fled into my dictionary
one page after *facetious*, I thought of you.

Words were my war weapon, no matter how much
you loved Dickens. All the names and words of endearment
I never called you, and you could never find in your dictionary
to call me, daddy, all the names of dearness, daddy, when I spat
at you in the street, and ridiculed you in public, joying at the response
to the ridicule, and my way with words as war weapons.
Daddy, when the word *hatred* sprang up in class or conversation,
daddy, you were top of the league, you were right beside the word.

And it rained.
And I love the rain, daddy, but you were never part of it.
I was out on the lawn, and it was rosy September.
Mother was addicted to wobbly eggs, and she made herself that way,
daddy, with your tremendous help. You were good at that, dad,
I give you that. Daddy, when the word *broken* fled into the
dictionary, daddy, your oleaginous self was there smiling
to give it a helping hand. Only you would have been there.

When *ostentation* fled to the hills into my upland notebook
I flaunted it right back in your direction, daddy. You knew what
it meant.

O goodness, daddy, I've dropped my dictionary,
and my knowledge of words and phrases, punctuation and properly-placed
full-stops, but I know I'm alright daddy. I can steer clear
of my stupid awfulness. You'll be there, daddy,
with a welter of words. With a punishment of punctuation.
Daddy, you personally placed the sin in syntax.

And I went to the Durham Family Practitioner Committee,
and they were very kind and told me straight, for straight
is what I need, dad, now that drink has twisted me.
One day, daddy, and this is what they said from the
bottom of their professional hearts. One day, with
rain from Sligo sheeting in the poor street, or
rain from the desolate areas of unkindly Strabane,
or from Denton Burn for that matter, or Waddington
Street, where my heart is in storage, in a furnace,
oddly enough, not in a freezer, or an ice-cube
tray (yellow, not transparent) – and don't forget
my dear da, don't ever forget. The French verb
is *oublier*, daddy – that when you sent your devil letter
your snide, sneering, you Demon With Knives In The Mouth,
daddy, when you posted it at 14:15 in the beautiful city
of Cambridge, a city that does not need your evil,
there is the letter, daddy, in the grate, where we
burned it, and when we did that, daddy, we burned you.

And when I had been to the Durham Family Practitioner Committee,
and it is housed in a marvellous building abutting the
Western Hill, and I cock my head at it always, and
when I had been to the vale, and all of the other hills
which lie in my soul, and their souls, and the souls
of all of those who have walked them and loved them
and hoped their souls and soulsongs would be collected and loved
by a poet who would always be scorned by his da, daddy.
I stood in the street at four in the day, itch of matins
and mitted palms over the river in the great cathedral.

I pondered it seemed almost forever upon the kinds
of factual annoyance you dislike, père, Mr Not Sit Him
On Your Knee, so I deliver it to you in this poem,
on my way back to the home of my great beloved, whom you
will never meet, evil devil daddy, even in the waiting room of the handsome

home of the Durham Family Practitioner Committee, who
told me, without saying one word, one verb, one sentence,
there were no subjunctive clauses or split infinitives
lying on the patients' area table, daddy, when they told me:

the rains of Sparty flower all the way from the ferry landings of
Ireland, from the land of spuds and stout, and pipes
and the great glens of poetry, Eileen Aroon and the loughs of swans
and swanning if you fancy on a very soft day, daddy. Let
me tell you how it is now – all the press releases have
been sent, and all those who received them in the world
of poetry and demons upstairs have shredded them and their faxes.
We are approaching the midday of the time of Nobody Zero, a time
of failed locks and pushed back chairs in a hurry.

It will rain, which is a day I love most, daddy. It will
pour and drip like a wound in the funny black sky. And I
will be in a badly repaired car in a field not quite the green
of the paint on at least one of the walls of the Durham
Family Practitioner Committee surgery in its handsome
building, daddy. And I think, daddy, that the car idling
on the sill of the soaking sike will be black too.
And I will hunch out of the driver seat, and
I will look at the rain and strangely enough be glad of the
rain. And this is what I learned, this is what my headwounds
and my heartstrips, and my little bookstrips were written on, pa,
da, daddy, père, this is what they told me in the red
wounds which are woven across me like very bad ribbons, daddy.

They were very reasonable, daddy, most personable,
no slyness involved, no letters unsigned posted in
Cambridge from the Headquarters of Insecure Fathers,
for that is what you are, daddy, after all, a father.
But believe me, the cheeky chappy behind you in the
miserable family photographs, you were never a father to me.
You were never a father and you were never a friend.

You saved my brother from drowning, daddy, you saved
your youngest son. O thank God, daddy. If you
can love a brother more than a brother, da, I love Paul.
Our Paul, da. But it is not enough to try and find a
redundant welder in the Durham Family Practitioner Committee
and after angry handshakes and solidarity exchanges
at the closure of another
worldwide great shipyard that I might in my poetic
unappreciated nightmare about you, daddy, ask for

227

flux to weld my utterly broken heart to yours in
some kind of common long lost at last agreement. I
cannot, daddy, I just cannot. The keys of my agelong
Olympia typewriter, my brilliant friend, which I carry with
me from here to there, all of those thousands of words
which I heaped against you one way or the other, for
hatred of you, or for lost love of you, and that you
never respected me for what I did.

And what they told me – and they did not know that they
had told me – in the Durham Family
Practitioner Committee, is that one day, daddy, one darkly liquid jewelled day,
I will stand

As the wind and western rain sweep from the Atlantic
into Strabane, I will bulge my shoulders, more used
to pushing open the off-licence door, bulge them
from the driver side window, all the time thinking of my beloved,
but let me tell you, daddy, what they told me, in between
the units leaflets, when I was reading them on the
badly-lit late bus going home, this is what they told me.

I would be getting out of the driver seat of the
poorly parked badly repaired car going home
in the sight of the bungalows, and they are always bungalows, daddy,
and the poorly repaired car is always black, da, it's
always black in a black spud-filled field, and always
a black day, or another Bloody Sunday, or any other
bloody bad day or month or year you dare to mention. And I will
get out of the car and I will heave my boots
across the turf and beyond the spuds, daddy,
do you remember, daddy, that's why we all left Ireland,
why we were always so envious of America, dadaddy, that's
why we were always so Popish proud, and it was raining,
belting down,
you know the rain, da, the rain we love so much, the soft rain
and the hard rain, on the rivers and hills, when we went fishing,
and it swept our very love away. And every day when we woke
it was there
as we walked up it was right in our faces.

And what they told me, was that I
will be almost half out of the black car, the Austin
A40, knee deep, god help me already, in the stricken wastes
of Crossmaglen and ugly Strabane, in the permanent borders
of crossfire, bull-horn warnings, rain-dulled crackle of

walkie talkies barely heard from soaking ditches, and the cross-hairs
of my heart, for this terrain, and terrain is all it is, a word with
a bleakness to it all of its own, despite a false disguise of green,
there my heart will be, steady as a drum for Billy, cold
as the kneecapping street on the outskirts, bizarre
as the surreal paintings on gable ends of those horse-riding men
in grand plumage and cockades.

Rain sheets down Hollywood-style, bigger than it is in nature.
No use hunching against it now. Collar up and the clava on and
right hand in pocket to make sure as the white-painted and pebble-dashed
bungalows worm out before me in their cheap mediocrity.
Rain their priceless diadem.

What goes through my cross-hairs heart at this time, in the final trudge,
are the beatings and berations, the betrayals of one who expected to
be loved. But then the ultimate repayment with thanks after the beltings
and verbal child abuse, when I sped up myself through sport and poetry
to be a robust youth with knockdown ideas of his own. And here was the
bungie, no more than a byre with net curtain, sidelights, bad carriage
lights, and leaden crossed porch torch as depicted on miscellaneous
false Yuletide postcards – and white oblong chime bell, which I pressed.
At least it was not Beethoven's Fifth and no dog barked: unusual.

All of that gunfire in the choke of the city, just over there. Orange
city council lights psychedelically flashed with Black and Tan
electric blue sweeps. We rocked like that in the sixties when we
fled from the various dictators and authorities. You for example, daddy.

A lad, a snow-haired cheeky chappy lad with little turned up smile
came to the door with eager I'll get it as he ran down the short hall
to the unsnecked chrome handle and yanked it in. Not more than seven,
just like the deadly sins, daddy, a wee white shirt, short pants and
Clark's sandals, eyes
still drugged with the wonders of what he had been reading in his
pocket *Aesop's Fables*. He wasn't daft at all. You could see the
awesomely distasteful glow of the red bulb imitation coal effect
from the living-room fire, and he ushered me in up the hall
the little snow-haired lad with hand outstretched inviting
me in from outside the pebble glass wind resistant door
as I felt in my pocket and asked him in a voice only loud
enough for him to hear:

Is your daddy home?

Angel Showing Lead Shot Damage

Let's dab a double finger half-pissed kiss on Muddy's lips. O
she's sixteen years old.
Tonight in the troubletorn heartland where heroes die and play,
in the knightly arenas of vainglory, demons' candle dancing
and lancing of the moon's throat will see us down
betrayed by feverfaith in love. Howl on, my pounding and delinquent soul
until her gunship
is taken up to tapers of the sunne.
Quenched ferocity, blanched faces turned indifferently
are all the twisted bee rave now.

My sleek torpedo will return, fins aflame
beneath the sheets. That's her promise.
Yet into blood I'm forged, bile and vomit
stranded in the fingers' stretch
                              where nurses cannot come
against demonic upheavals of villainous
dread night.

Here the poet will die, pickled and puce.
Dead man walking theme tune.
Number 13 tattooed on his neck.
Beast caged behind frail and fragile bars.
So when loose
it rips the very forest to an hilarity of shreds, bones
and burns
to join her scalding kisses
just a Canon automatic click away.
She is an angel sure, a privy perle
                              set rod-high
against all pestilence, needle and nag.
Rotten boroughs
of wine and gin
by the busload, look out!

In the land of wet brain and liver dysfunction,
subscriptions for coffin not necessary.
Messrs Demon and Sons see to everything.
And one last gargle before the screws
are twisted in.

Shreds Of Mercy/The Merest Shame

Shunned, ignored, cast off, slung in the bin,
sent from the bridge, pariah man, Mr Negative Endless,
fiercely fingered out by his ice queen and put on ice:
Gazer at photographs, kindler of memories hung on the wall.
But there's no breathing hot reality here today!
You lean, arms out east west, on the powerful rivetted
spine of our Malevich Suprematist bridge, above
the raging salmon spawning greatest river, but
it is only a picture, and the sky is moonmilk blue.

Today it's me with the twelve strings, the three
bars, me with the solo harmonica, unaccompanied
raw heart sax machine. Me with the loony frets.
No more us the boon fruits. Me Disney Dumbo big ear re-make.
Big ones, plopping pear drops splash on the silent pathways.
Always the salinations, cheek wiping, straight up
from the human salt beds. What matter this? *Don't ever leave me.*
Harmless nightdressed Palladium utterance
it really seems. Yet it blows like thunder
crushing at least one fucked up skull.
When it pops out of my enzyme count I'll sign for it,
if write I may and can. Don't bank on it, as in bank.

My great hero Kazimir Malevich, how the moon the other night
was just like your Suprematist plate in 1917, when
you quietly stormed the waiting world
with your railway sidings. I wear a cap in honour of you.
Now I have my CAFE CUBANO – Tueste Oscuro, and
today, with the rosemary flowers so azure
beneath the borage heavens, I,
like you, and Sergei and Vladimir, hate
all of my replicant oppressors, double-breasted
faces, Otis lift tunes all of the way to the boardroom if you fancy.
And Kazimir, I think of your wonderful plate, wonderful
is not too great a word to use. Indeed, it is undervalued
these very salination days, these days of liver expansion.
And Sergei, and Vladimir, I think of your guns,
and what they can eventually do. I used to myself shoot one,
but never at myself, though I have always had reason.

Yes, bless, blessure, bliss and blood, worst and wine
are my saintly, thorny words. I am crowned by them!
Not wearing fur-fringed gloves upon her flinty fingers

231

which sometimes taxed my shifting planets, she
felt my collar, for I am a drunken criminal of overspent
love, and she threw me in the jail of my terrible life.
Always in the locker of my single-minded lit-stricken cuffs
reaching for the emerald glass cylinder
cork within aperture, and the demons rampant
in their crest cockiness hands down my throat.
Hysterical psychotic drain cleansers.

In With The Stasi

Gnashed fervour licks down like fire
as the diazapam takes over and I lurch worse than drunk
down the locked ward. Barred windows, bedlam,
and all that mashed potato. I am mashed
also, stale holocaust bread without milk.

The autumn leaf which blows its tiny way
through the wonderful universe
before streams sweep it into nowhere.

No milk, just water with the dosage, urine. No wine.
But that is the curse of the Demon who shall always
be known as The One With the Mouth filled
with Rustling, Restless and Relentless Blades.
The wine comes complete with salt! Drink
at your own expense, but lap that brine. Suck
the Dead Sea dry and imagine it best burgundy.

In the hospital, locked and barred in the Harding Ward,
up the redbrown carpet into the first floor mental asylum,
away from the ground floor ward of patients under section,
with a blue carpet, with a phone, as in telephone, booth
working, first charge 20p, 10p not enough, 10p to
the red telephone company and 10p to the new trust,
which frankly seemed minimal, even the most heroic
twig of my family's tree died for want of mashed spuds
in Cork on the blanket on a prison bedbunk, it's all
on the gravy train of pills down the dry throat
and the mashed taties a comforting white collar.

I was not there to hold his hand when he died for
freedom and he was not in bedroom 4 to hold mine
when very funny vermilion lines slide viper-like
up the wall escaping the ant-gangs gathering to
plan a throat-choke raid on me at 4.50am.

Knocked up at 7 for the showers, the brain-dumbing
first knock-out of the day, the tick-off from Mr Starched
White Coat with Himmler clipboard, then the shit-brown
bran after a look at the slumped pink cardies to see
if death had come upon them yet. We tumble to
The Trough and exchange our troubles. And when we,

except Tony, dying from self-imposed malnutrition
and not from any kind of certifiable brain disease,
and who was from a village sacked by the shock troops
of this present Government, and not even on a proper
glucose drip, sitting on his bed in Bedroom Four, and
when we, not to repeat to even test your listening boredom,
sank back pill-brained and detoxing into bed, I
knew why in 1994 the windows were still iron-barred.
No corpses to be found on the York stone flags please
or it would have meant deducted funds on April Fools Day.

Pasolini Demon Memo

The Jesus Christ Almighty is a barely stripling bare-chested biker.
Bolting Pharisee jailers shaking shackles and chains, knuckled
love and *hate* in Galilee blue, ace of clubs across his tanned blades.
He rides into town on a Vincent Black Shadow and moves his feet around.
My territory, his territory.
But we won't fight it out. We won't do a Hemingway.
We'll exchange bike parts, accelerating road stories
and little-known facts about best oil and chrome polish.
In our eyes we can both see it: no curses or cures, both
on a dustbowl highway leading to the cleansing of temples
and the unstrapping of my Goliath gargle gargantuan addiction.
He had telling things to say and I had mine. Townsfolk
arced around in an awe of wariness and dread, planning
all mock trials ahead.
He had a cross to go to
and I have mine.
O yes, let's kick some Makem Pharisee
scruffs from the thrash-hot main drag
handing in all badges and spreading allegiance to nobody.
Together let's beat the smotherers of justice.
Fill her up, load her up, ready to run.
Your blood's fluxed with serious innocence and grace,
but my tongue tells me I need something stronger.

Ferocity?
Try me my provoked and peppery friend.
Meanwhile, until the thunder rolls
and the street becomes a bloodbath,
come inside and lean against the bar.
Red wine for you, gin for me,
as the menfolk shrink away.

Later we'll listen to the eternal music of plovers.
You'll meet Pearl and her unremitting ceaseless silence.

I'll tie one on, ready for a vomit seizure
alone in the treeline.
Expecting an overcooked cauliflower brain
convulsion, a horizontal twitch dance in the locoweed.
Addicted to alcohol, poet away with the prairie fairies,
the monkeys and the demon mixer.

Ignore me and the medics arriving
stuffing the bottle down a gopher hole.
Stick around.
You'll make sheriff one day.

Nil By Mouth: The Tongue Poem

Demons, big-hatted and hard-hatted, far as gutter-toppled
squint-eye with grapple-lost spectacles can see, custard brain
head slanty on kerbside perch, vomit ready for a roller ride
into the X-rated, dog arse emptying unlit street, mongrel eyeing
the demon conveyors from here to eternity, bottle after bottle,
twisted cork to twisted head and unscrewed, screwed-up life,
over the slag heap of stonegrey aggregate from the moony saltpan
beds where the stones will surely lie upon my swollen liver,
as the swollen argent river sweeps across the tumblestones.
Grog demon biceps leaving me moan groggy, foggy-bonced,
pouring lunarstruck salt, sel de mer, coarse white pellets
scuttle-funnelled on MacSweeney's stuck-out begging tongue:

Tongue stuck out like raw begging hand in the mall, sticking
out straight, single digit filthy message signal up yours tongue,
in the air bloated for booze upright needle Cenotaph tongue,
grovelling, whining, soliciting, pleading, eyes imploring,
thirst, thirst, thirst, craveache, pinecovet, itchneedlust,
but on comes the salinating, saliva-droughting insult, Sahara
mouth an agony O, my Lot's wife tongue, rough orange fur tongue,
tongue examined by Dr Guo in needle room number two,
bladderwrack tongue late of the ebbingtide pools, salt on the rocks,
tongue of the deep sea trawler lick hull clean department,
tongue out on rent as a dog's public park hard-on, for
artists to paint in glory of its pinky stiffness and quality
as blotting paper for anything as long as it's a double on the rocks.

Blot, blot, blot, blotting me out: moan, moan, take me
from the slake tide to lake or snaky clean river, before
the endless chained pails of salt end me, tireless demons
happy in their work: a regular seven dwarfs scenario,
whistling darkly all the way to the daily saltbeds as
they pour, pour, pour, and the demons' capped gaffer,
fancy Dan Demon Man, who shall always be known as
the one with the Mouth of Rustling and Relentless Blades,
swaggers barely into focus from my throne in the gutter,
one hand filled with bottles and the other with scran.

Just one more, sir, for the road?

Demons In My Pocket

Arrest me asleep, crashed out
under the eye of the borage: So what? I'm
just pissed as a primrose posy
beneath an April shower. I'll do.

At least I'm speaking in cogent sentences
from the back of nowhere below an argent moon.
At least I'm not a replicant Labour Party goon.
I sold my fancy suits for vodka and a copy

of The Russian Experiment in Art.
It was the only way I could get near
Kazimir. I stood proud alone
in the Stalingrad rain and read

the legend headlines: Fiend Poet
Shot Dead With Broken Hat. Scald
Of The Steppes Before Firing Squad
Accused Of Dawdling On Lithic Tuff

With Shattered Socialist Heart – Gun
Seized. Friend Of Few Flees Not So
Lengthy Life With Unpunished Book.
But they were all too long or badly

bust and the typeface choice at least
debatable. So much in my oddly spring-
like foreign guises – Swanne, Ludlunatic,
MoonySwooney, Madstag, Lenin Wolfboy or

swiftly skilful terrace tantalising
push and run teaser fan pleaser Sweeno –
I yearned for 200-point Cyrillic caps
across seven cols or in cirrus strands

and to be a bloodred flower too, guts &
heart upon my sleeves and not a pinko posy!
Not to be out in rainy Nevsky Prospekt
but here I am at the back of nowhere

under a fickle sickle harvest five-year
plan pearly Shirley shiny moon, dreaming
in my railway sidings way of tiny toes
and teeming tumblestones twined without

torment in greeny locks and coronets
of cushy crushed footfall meadow cowslips. In
the dimmed and dimming day when it
will be dark along the river and always

dark and Othello will pad freely demented
a panther in my sickened heart, I feel
the gutter twisting, hard-fortuned
carrier of water and nitrates to the

unholy earth, and it all, all, yes, all
of it, howls in the basement bowels as
the gale gets up its fatal goat. Starlings
thrash the sky at dawn in feathered

shoals, quitting nightrest rooftop
cat-free safety of the city centre Odeon.
Truly, I do have 20/20 Vision: She's
gone, she's gone, but what can I do? What

drives me to you is what drives me
insane. Mental rental idiots in hatred
uniform pursue me through fire
escapes to arrest once and forever

before the racing sails of my heart
can capture her eyes of borage blue.
They'll drag me away from B&Q the
gall and spite and malice crew, to

filthy demon paperwork and drinkwork,
to slurword work, collapse hardwork,
to tonguebite drudgery *grand mal* jerkwork
and far away, my fingerfast, from you.

All my rotten reeking shrieking shreds
are speaking fast now, sledging off my
funnybone tongue. The very last words
sung, they're exploding and expanding

as they hit the croaking creaking rhizome
rats' tail ground. Outbreak! Outbreak!
Thousands dying and thousands dead! It's
more an incurable curse than a human

tempest clashing in the midnight blue
of the outer outskirts of Murmansk.
All human malevolence planned, sewerage,
invade my hair and lips and lovely

blue far horizon cloud cotton-soft eyes.
Killer virus in my brain bane, this liquid
poison potion passion pestilence for which
I have shown so little prayerful penitence

coughs its infection into my lovely kitten
drunken face. Spikes, brads, studs and welds
bussed up the bombed-out road from Nixville
to empty eager waiting bottle-holding hands.

Nailbite squall-stirring helicopter gunships
of darkest green – it is dark now along the
moonless river and dark and always dark –
descend to drop the flogging hammers in.

Tell Anne she can have her wildest pills
again tonight and the devil be on look-out.
My rattlechain hands go out unshaking now
in feverfew frenzy, big Russian tarragon

twister tornado as it whips its Monroe hips,
in the hostile thunder bellow days alone away
from you my lovegun, my bullet to the heart.
The violence universal of all you warders,

white coats or blue: needle room number two,
Chinese doctor grinning at me Manchurian
Candidate with her needles and punctures,
bars or no bars, mashed spuds or no spuds.

In single mode I speak out clearly astride
the argent turquoise starre system which
beams in your eyes. No log-in further
sequence needed. To log-out now means to die.

And the terrible gutters move again aching
with gargoyle gushing rain above the graves
dug by those who will lie in them horizontal.
The moon's awesome gaping craters lean in

and the lurid savage cranberry sunne muscles
up inside its squadron of burning over and above
the iceblue rims of the fabulous fjords. Is that
Kazimir, John or Percy in the railway sidings

astride or in or beneath or moving through
the water? It is the streaming dark water,
for the water is dark and it is always dark
and the night is dark and cold is the very ground.

The emerging lanceheads of the chives are so
beautiful tonight, by offshore rigs, mainland
bridges and cranes, and humans walk beneath
the stars by the streaming dark water where

in the land of tumblestones it is dark and always
dark. Hear the roots of the flowers stress even
the mighty earth and cry. Feel the mad planet
buckle at the soul and knees. This memo to all:

I am 72-inches tall, yet when I go to meet John
and Percy and Kazimir and Pearl, stick me in
an oven and burn me just the same. Then I will
be a true Jew, a poet through and through.

The Horror

The horror of the hospital for us both.
Demolished eager hopes and trudges up the bad
steep hill in your dun winter clothes: to be
refused information. Not your bright red
party jacket not your guitar badge and
funny pinned on chrome figure. Just
petitions and pleas – how's that man
of mine? That badly displaced fellow
on 50 mils a day and what, what for
god's sake, is he eating, and I don't even
believe in gods – or that one from
Cecil B. De Mille. For when the Wall,
and I don't mean the tourist attraction
touted in China, when the Wall was
chipped to bits it broke my stern heart
and it broke his, my man, and I know
you are breaking his and mine now.

And you are breaking me to uphill
trudge bits and episodes – like poor
hammered toffee – and I cannot eat
myself and I am being distracted
my heart itself once an oven of love
turned into a rainy asylum alone
in the bleak upland rains. How
much better it might be in summer,
recovering our seasons released
upon sensational sun-peeled skin,
boats and oars and oarlocks and
handlocks and kisslocks locked
right in place, pure juice from
Spanish oranges, Miró suns pouring
endless light over grief of my walk
across the spated river, touching
the black painted bridge lamp after
dark, made in Brum, near where
Nazi airmen torched my childhood
cathedral; me in a shelter, afraid
of flames and fire, as you are now,
flames in your heart, O darling
don't let them be extinguished now,
it is the smashed cathedral of your
life sweeping up in utter flames

to the frozen ground: torched and
charged with terrible destruction.

For many days, my man, you were
a man with a many-layered mask.
You did not want to know me and
again as I arrived and arrived you
bent your head and heart away and
did not want to know me. My own
heart a haunted husk without you.
But always I put my hand out and
want to and always did and do. We
have been driven to distractions
by a long revelation of deprivation
madness which triggered me to
trudging, loving you, pursed lips
grim in every worried step back
to your haloed bed in wardlight.

Your northern arms around me
not browned by Miró's molten suns,
and you held me strong and lovingly,
northern hands, tight, tight, tight,
forearms around my ribs and spine,
making me shudder in happiness
and unbroken realms of loving safety,
so paleness of spirit left me undaunted;
a queen of hearts and a warrior of love!

Yet once more I am at the hospital door.
Once more you will be completely
off-centre and pilled up, caustic tongue
not lazy. Once more betraying my heart
your illness clinging like oak-roots.
I pray the trees will lend you strength.
The time has come to palm aside all
images of lost sheep and willows weeping.
In my bad dream you climbed to the wet
roof of the lunatic asylum, through barred
windows, determined to be demon free.
You said you were a magpie and would
fly to me. But your flight ended in a fatal
swan-dive into the Yorkstone yard. O
mendacious reel of bad fortune, let
sun's pollen-gold wake me to a saner world
so fleet already without this torment too.

Demons Swarm Upon Our Man And Tell The World He's Lost

Smartism seems to be the best deal
in these broken-fire days, honed up
with barely held apologies, not the
Suprematism of monumental Kazimir.
He'd weep seven broken plates at its
purity of abjectness, lack of muscle
tone. Not for us now to stand upon
the steps in a revolution's moment,
with Miró's crown of sun and stars.

All the demonic graffiti is quite certain:
    I'm the abjuring man.
    I'm the abdicating man.
    I'm the strangely dislocated
    disconnecting disconnected man.
    I'm the storm-tossed tosser
    on Earthquake Street, mindblown
    dead on arrival sprawled on
    Richter Scale Prospekt, found
    crying wolf beside the troikas.
    I alone in detox itch and fury
    test the temper of sunbeams
    and angels. I flee across the shiny
      floor – believe me, it is shiny –
    headbackward pursued by flying
     animals and objects each
       with forktail cocktail blazing. Endless anger
      only is my recompense for
       first-rate pistolage now she's
      fled these shores for sanity.

    O my wires keep dropping out.
    Let loose my stumble in the darkness.
    Fling my face into brooding earth.
    Trample forward onto footloose ground.
    Watch the devil's tarpit veil smother me.
    Who today will fetch my idle drinkless
    hands a king whose neck wants wringing?
    Who will set me free from strapdown
    to deliver Sexton's necessary utmosts?
     It will be the last house-call after all.
     No, no, it is all drinkless dole and drollery,
    regime of hysterical tomfoolery.

Why can't you get helium on the National Health?
Because the Tory Government has taken it all.
It is dispensed every day to Cabinet ministers.
Now they are gone completely myxomatosis bunny funny.
May the demons track them down
as they tracked me. Relentless pursuit
and capture their family's fantastic method
code and motto. O, SAS where are you now?
Gone to an alcohol oasis every one.
Blackhand gangs through every window
leapt craving my wit from ice-wagons – every day
was Drink More Pour More Day.
May they sting their heads and hearts
and sap their very strength and breath.
Am I alone in my symmetrical vision
of this unequivocal stupidity? Look
at the Labour Party too & roar with laughter.
All, all, all, clowns of conceit.

Shafted & driven intolerant on spewground
wearing only an orange Cuba baseball cap
say then this: Lift one much exercised
right arm more used to shifting Russian
vodka, drunkenly saluting naked and badly
bruised Albion and that failure St George,
declaring in soaking mattress rawness –
that's the ugly nation you have made.

And that's the nation of me too: each of us
in very separate parts brought to our knees.

Hooray Demons Salute The Forever Lost
Parliament Of Barry And Jacqueline

Now it is time to put aside and forget
the decadent period of fast red cars &
slothful attitudes towards boldness
and moral mettle except in entering
the National Lottery, the greatest
con yet wrought by the Tory Party –
worse than cheap gin for quelling
here in the Great United Quelldom
where tomorrow never comes fast
enough for win ticket announcement.

I have been admiring the caked
menstruation blood you left
on a pillow before we parted.
It was the most tender
moments of our days.
We laved and laved the blood away
and you helped me with my broken leg.
It's amazing what we did considering.

Nothing remains now.
World in smithereens.
4:56, sun rising after me,
swoon alone in the garden
at lilac and azalea fumes
thanking heaven inside
the utter madness for
nasturtium you planted
before fleeing from
my darkriver drinking.

Rain, alone in the rain,
rain and the train and
the river darkly summoning
towards its source my heart.
All the buttercoppes
flush like forests ankle-high.
I am so glad to live at the
northern end of the earth!

The south would suffocate
and humiliate me. Once more
the blossoms and birds. Even
aconite and horehound
bloom and bloom. I&I

myself am in a poisoned
corner, Chatterton-style,
entirely deconstructed.
Toe pressing the mad earth.
Stiff bottom lip turned out
against the rules and rest
of it, all in despotic shame.

Said: should do, but I won't.
And she said: that's the story
of your life. Almost man.

When The Candles Were Lit

Rain, rain, rain again and bonerolling bloodthunder,
    lampblack clouds from the Pennines
        towards fjords in the east
          releasing their load
  soaking the tied-back crown of Russian tarragon, swaying
        so high in the herb garden
          – reminding me
  of the cast-back hair of Anne de Bretagne in 1514
commemorated in marble: full-length along the sealed casket
eyes closed by human hand, lips half-parted for a last kiss,

      O please, O please beloved,

    and those frontal bones and ribs pushed up
    made more emphatic in her exit exhalations
    in the Cathedrale Basilique Saint-Denis
        as the young beauty
      longed to find her breath.

     Yes, Paris, you have everything,
      the fastest nitrate in the best Laforgue rain,
      the best gutters and downpipes and poets
    and the marble hightide hair swept back in death pose
       like wind-whipped tarragon.

Pearl Against The Barbed Wire

How sweet today the scents and air perfumes
down the overgrown flags, binding stems
cling to my fair descending legs
which never saw a proper dance
in the arms of another – at village gatherings
I could only nod, neither saying
yes or no. So charmless harmless me!

Yet the true blue cranesbill like heaven's light, invading
our brilliant path at Sipton Shield, crowning
the riverbed of tumblestones, is my
queenly ankletwine today, and the Michaelmas
which will be for my hair, washed
in the white water, crown of hair
lashed back from my supple neck, O yes
I hoy it back, defiant almost, if I knew
the word defiant and I wished I did know,
for it is a gunmetal word with a hard 't'
all should be acquainted with, with which all
should be in talking agreement: talking, what's that
my sky-blue eyed Bar?
You speak the petals off the trees
each day and I in wonder
watch you draw them down. You're like a bird
with fluting beak, while the silence
of the Nenthead shafts populate
with lack of noisesomeness my full
disabled cleft and tongue.

To call me idiot, brand me nobody,
is bestowing lustrous ermine qualities
upon my nowhere frame. There are no proper words for me.

Pearl: now our secret paths above the tumblestones
are pierced by yellow arrow marks
for all of those who would walk there too.

Everybody's tortured, everyone's in chains.

I hate them and loathe them with strengthening abundance,
forehead-strong, and when my abundance, my overflowing
emotion, my abundance of the heart, my
moorland affluence and wealth which others call poverty,

when it streams like a fire seam,
I loathe them for binding my pearly toes.

I hate them because I am among their
other refugees. They put up the wire, wire, wire,
along my way,
which no one should do, for wire
is an industry, a containment, made in
Leeds or Wakefield Bar said, brought by 12-wheeled lorries
in unrolled bales like silver hay
from some industrial graveskin graveyard
completely contrary to the wings of my spirit.

Fraught I am with poor lip service,
destroyed and betrayed
and the river flows from me, my molten white water,
1500 to 1400 to 1300
                              past hawhips and sloes
and so to the sea.
I will wash myself in it forever.
Darling, reader and writer with azure eyes,
eyes the colour of the sea's horizon,
I will wash myself in it forever.

In umber spate it ripped my breastbuttons, like your eager hands.
It broke apart my loving heart, like your cruel talking lips.
It stopped my sense.

O love, in a world of shuffled papers
and cheap haircuts, your honeysuckle-
scented locks, your locked and gripped
tongue will always be delight to me. In
an alien world of distant characters,
you'll always be inside the dangerous
part of my forever welling willing heart.

Bar, Bar, barbed wire. Bar, the barbs
and staples and hooks and eyes. Did
you see the photographs? Did you see
the charred skin, the gravedigging
ceremony with gleaming boots,
spectacles and sneery smiles?

Did you take note my angel poet
of the complete famine due to
circumstances beyond control
of let's grin and bear it?

Did you see the bushels of knees
and other thinly-appointed limbs
and the gaps of extracted – there's
a word, my Bar, I know you'd love –
teeth, did you wonder where the world
was, where the world went, my honeysuckle love?
Blonde but a Jewess just the same.
No one had our words in those days.

When we stared and wandered
and stored and wondered
in each others' far-reaching eyes

beneath the croaking creaking tumblestones
where our trout leapt mad for midge and mayfly
pollen puffed in gold explosions by sucking bees,

our ankles smoothed to Oriental beauty, before
either of us knew where was the Orient, before
Jeremy travelled there, before you read me

Fu-Manchu and the Yellow Peril, O dimmer
of my heavy lids, dizzy with pollen and sunlit
prose, O stunning quiet reader, seducer

of pathside petals and birdy wings, bringer
of betony, pointer out of fairies' chimneys,
runner of rings in the rinsing rain.

I stood in any light there was, in
every light, dark and almost dark,
fiercely black, like a dark heart torment,
strangely grey all the way all day
from the storm-shaken ferry jetties of Ireland,
and I stood there, arms, heart and mouth open,
ready to be annoyed and poorly-addressed
by the sudden sun over the longing of the law,
and ready to be addressed by my loving love.

Medici? Three syllables, my honeysuckle
tumblestone rosehip love, but I did not
feel like an Italian court princess, for
my vowels were uncut marble then.

Even writing the words *rose* and *garment*
broke my heart; their real variousnesses
pricked me awake when I expected it least.

O my love, my rosehip plucking love, my love,
kiss the bandage from my face and haul me from the wire.

All the mam-made hems, the man-made hymns,
none of the blood-filled truths, none, I say none,

none of them can move or call me as you can.
O my love, my harping, high fell honeysuckle

tumblestone molten white water love, haul me
from the terrible terror of the wristblood wire.

Nothing Are These Times

I am gnawing jawface, furman, odd cove
alone in the tree-line, pawpoison back
of the track pack, blood beneath the rolling

mills of sense, MC for this mad filthy earth
whose prancing demon gaffers have me
straight between the shoulder blades

and down the garglevomit hole they call
a throat. I am the bloatstoat, floating
volevoter at the collapse pollstation.

Each bouncer's waistcoat gemstarred
with fragments of Bunting Betelgeuse.
Utterly I say in the dark and demon cup:

was it not brokenwing swanlove on
the rocks which left us forlornly grieving?
Do parts of your brain go guavapulp?

Or do you just become another child-
belting father and repeat the mistake?
Does hand-wringing become a new habit?

Fierce broken light arrives in the sky
shaded by a linen shawl of Irish winds:
beating demon daddies for once seem far away.

All gulpdragons have me by the breath
& my broken heart a wretched drumbeat
now you have swanned aloft in his arms.

Sleepless nights, stalk fever in my shoes.
Bad crack, smack, nerve gas and Tarzanjuice.
Pharoah's army nurses come right in

smiling like the greetings card Jesus
in the fairytales. We're their broken bread,
their human weeds, not flowers on

the pearly path to Jerusalem. If it isn't
up the nose, it's down the head-drain
or in the skin. Anyway it's death & death's

delay button with shaky finger on it.
And we're here in the eternal land
of sensible branflake breakfasts

with UHT crap semi-skimmed clarts
from France. We hated it even more
than we loathed ourselves, each nailed

to the fantastic frantic demon tree.
Yes, it's the best the council can manage
and it's a bright hole and nothing at all.

Friends, fellow non-members of the
black sun anarchist nada addict group:
we're in for a lousy final chapter.

No end in sight in starry bruisy night.
Bad bus one way to Snowville.
Forgiveness sold out no longer available.

Dead Man's Handle

(after a word by Mayakovsky)

Comb the crawling morning chill chilling sky in search for vodkafire.
Forgive me my combing, forgive me my crawling, forgive me my fire.
The blue sky, the blue cold sky.
Forgive me, forgive me, forgive me, my kisses now lost opportunity.
Forgive me for the cold blue sky painted in your eyes.
Forgive my knee-bending
when I pleaded with you to forgive me, forgive me,
transforming your face into a planet for kisses, forgive me my lipkeen leaning.
The spangled sky with no gods in it, forgive me for not giving you gods
and the very moon a humble eye reflecting our folly, forgive me my folly
as we walk here in the windstrewn gravity defence league posture department
destroying all that is dearest
all that is best to already broken hearts. Forgive me my heart,
my clownhearted tidal wave heart, forgive me my heart.
Picasso's peace dove just a pullet with broken craw,
dead olive twigs choking its throat. Not even worth eating, forgive me its
                                                    breaking.
The whole world a cubist disaster waiting to happen.
That cracker Jack crept in and killed the begonias with his winter switchblade,
forgive me his knife-edge.

Christmas is here and there'll be no summer.
Tomorrow really has arrived already and there'll be no today.
We walk apart in the night
and it may as well be continents
disproving history
                                        that swannes mate for life.
It's no life but a blank sheet again, all watercolours washed out in the rain
which was our growing season. Rainbow even
& soup by a lake.

Now it's dreadful and filled with dread.
Forgive me the black city which burns in my heart.
Listen to the crashing windows from the burning black cathedral,
the blazing jetblack cathedral of my broken heart.

Here comes the dazzling darza drinks-at-the ready
DEMONSPIEL:

the trophy is poisoned
                                        electric blue
all manners gone from the window

Go then, go back, go back to the halls of hell
go back to the single toll of the bell
go back, return, turn back to the empty bed
or the bed a linen scrapheap shaken by illusory sex for one miserable night only
then the deft departure at dawn, sly handsome fish through the net, the weeping,
the illusion
of coherence
the dream of integration
all the tables in the halls of hell

alive with broken jigsaws,
fragments, pieces, worse than Paddy's Market, heart ripped out again
sad in its bowing, alone in its screaming & dreaming

driven from heaven, screwed down and abandoned
in the windswept yawning tunnels within the halls of hell

go then, to your pillow of nails,
go then, to your coldfeet unmatched boats
go then, no ruddy waterfall of leaves on our tree
go then, sober & seeing everything so damned Warwickshire clearly
go then, to the solo crystal vision of yourself

These 252 mile an hour headlong thoughts towards the station and platform
at the final appearance of the jammed dead man's handle:

Always
gutterbright
to sky's light

the eternal gift
of starres

last train to Demonville right on time.

Himself Bright Starre Northern Within

(for J.H. Prynne)

There is absolutely no record
of goodness in the history of my soul.

I say delete world delete her dollypops,
delete great gulp Adam's apple Eveorange
delete all fancy her fingers throat-gripping
delete four winds sixteen windows
delete all the sad memories the torn books daddy
delete he with belt and Charlie Dickens
in his own privately-owned bad big Bleak House.
My house in the great city, my heart, my single solo
overture, over to the lightning-begging trees.
Delete memories, no memory for them
scattered, only one execution, not enough:
we did not cleanse
we did not feed the greenwood tree.
We flew aloft naked, one second only
not trusting the present: delete
the whole future dolldoodle dollywobble,
breastbabe delete dalliance Sun Alliance.

Dance dancing in the street delete
delete mugshots handcuffs social work aftercare
all known germs in cell fungus caught on spider carcase –
delete persons unknown teeth taken
spectacles and shoes piled high to the sky

delete all bank records of Nazi gold

delete the Swiss
and Zurich accountants
delete client confidentiality: we won't tell you who went
to the ovens
          who sank beneath the brainbullet, the pointed Luger
at wrist's interface delete delete

the JUDEN window the smashed starre

delete the flogged animal
alone in byre's blackness
delete the gas through ten shower holes
delete the savaged champion horse

257

delete the wordstation *forgiveness*
to be logged in by a nobody person not one
delete

I say delete midnight, midnight lawstarres, Pearlwords,
the mojo moon, no executed kings tonight, never enough,
delete kisses, poutlips, fast breasts, all the once-couple talk.

Ban delete all big skies Northumberland Texas to Samarkand.
All soft mouths, no salmon facedown in the pools, poisoned wraps
& wrappettes, down my legs in the tumbledown lone stones.

Forever. Delete all stolen slate from Nichol's byre nail fingers,
no fashion book available, no delete kisses button. Press it.
Delete all beautiful hand-made stone walls. All wonderful swanne quillpens.

Jibesneers, delete, citric fake mouths, sad eyes masking
erection false pledges and bounced vows, refer to drawer.
Extracted teeth with no anaesthetic. Then to the ovens,

just like a book or Jew. Publisher it was thee, you.
Delete longing I will not long for her up in the tree-line. Delete plaid
woven Tunisian brought-home blankets I will not lay a bed for her.

She reversed me my heart, she deleted me in very bad favour.
Delete sunne I won't smile in it the photographed poet upland bonny
lad. Never. I will not I won't I won't ache especially for her.

She's a distant thing. It's a special promise – I won't ache for her.
Each daw dawn in the argent slipstream I lie alone I won't ache for her.
When Mars goes to bed and I lie on my left side I won't miss her a forlorn
trance of Germany starres, I'll kill my lips for telling lies.
Delete Parliament, delete pushiest pout, delete plover west window.

Paul Celan, Paul Celan, Paul Celan, Paul Celan, nothing left to bruise.
Did you see the ovens, did you smell the awesome awful gas?

I was in the so-called shower and it rained right down on me.
I was so impressed I almost goose-stepped my way to the very front.

Delete all swinging wands of the wild fell rose, no more headlong chases

stalking the pearl moon which tonight is a broken opal crescent
delete all clocks put back at midnight in the soaring pouring rain

delete A1 crash victim Catherine through Land Rover windscreen
dead on arrival Morpeth wrapped in steel & glass after Wagner concert

delete her roadside brains long camelhair coat long late bus smiles
her fast clicking shoe heels speeded and rinsed with Northern rain

delete her forever lingering grin soon to be ruined & smashed completely
facedown in a lay-by body crushed and crumpled like Christmas paper

delete rain on the border at Hawick, delete beautiful rain in Glasgow
delete the soft water of Scotland, the proud taps, brilliance everywhere

clean drops dazzle off the cone-ends, off the sleeve-catching branches
how eyeful it all is up here in the uplands, delete all nonsense, delete good sense

proper behaviour delete upstanding citizen, terminate, erase, abolish,
abrogate, annihilate, very late, annul, cancel, cease, destroy, efface,

excise, negate, obliterate, literally omit, so close to vomit, one letter only.

Our eyelashes flicked silently and closed together down the middle of
Platform Two. I was a rich entrancing beast fulled with rampant bloode.

Hands, four of them, delete. Please dad I'm only seven don't hit me.

Stop beating me over the head. All I wanted was to write a poem, I
really don't know why. It just came to your son a lad in the windrow,

out of the snowfells out of the badly described sky. I know I'm an uphill
wanderer, a poor citizen, a republic of tents, springwater my fancy & Pearl.

See how I delight in it, you're so disappointed daddy that you cannot
control me. That, even at seven, is my eternal wish. My biggest dish.

Look where we walk up a height & raining & the flame-tipped trees.
Delete the chough the lark in the fastcut meadow.

Beware me in thunder.

Look at the buttercoppes down in the meadowbank, so yellow
as I look again into my craving craven heart. I'm the hound inside

your head, the suddenly-stiffening corpse in your bed, the long and lengthy
beads of dread, right up here in the heather-glad Highlands, my lands,

I will walk where the plover walks. Hold to it, stick to it. Be faithful
to the very cause. I will forever be the Silver Shadow, the grey shadow

standing tall & silent alone in the gardens beneath a silky opal moone.
This severe thing, hard time knowing, delete hard time, sounds like Dickens,

just a note penned in darkness, darling, trying to delete this severe thing,
trying to replace the whole complete person, the whole complete poem.

I will never ever wear three hats in one day ever again. Had hair then.
Delete reality and endless punishment, O Daddy please don't beat me.

I'll be as big as Charlie Dickens one day in my big lonely Elvis Orbison heart.
I was quite alone in ruthless daylight, fastly sinking under an argent moone.

Upcoming I saw the sunne, saw the light of heaven in a toilet roll.
I looked at the yellow toilet roll – thinking it the sunne – & beheld its gaze.

What happened to my incredible fantastic endless lovely fargone literacy?
All you end up with is Pound's petals on a wet black bough. Two lines.

Delete. Beware, beware, the shredded torn paper of the silver starres.
Delete all Pearls, beware, the cat's in the bag and the bag's in the river.

Emily your crystal vision – the Soul has bandaged moments –
delete the bite the ever-holding smitten grip, between your tongue & discreet lips:

You yourself bright starre, unbroken in the petty fetters,
delete her hairbun, when will you come in with Anne Sexton

to see if I'm still alive? I'm depending on both or either of you.
Listen Em: I like your solitude. Anne is drunk like me & far too rude

and useless unreliable. She's in bed too late. Drugs, drink, mad sex.
One of you betrayed everyone, not you Em with your cheeky sparklespecks.

It's just not you: it's more New York than New England.

Where in heaven is my timeless bride?
Where is she in her beautiful glide

to the frozen bathroom at 3 in summer
at 7am in the falling January snow?

I'll lie there alone and never, never know.
Pang in the mouth I am terrified of Ireland,

more so than the broken-down collapse of England,
because in the Republic Finnbar would be found out

for what he is. Guzzler, collector of demons, bar
snaker, Baggot Street crawler, hater of Poseurs.

Three bubbles in the glass of Jesus juice,
every single glass, Aislinn, one more after the other.

I stood on the edge of the world once, not caring,
there was a woman in white before my eyes went black.

Before my hurrying down throat became swollen & bruised.
I'll never be your flame. I'll never be your flame in a bush.

Ash, I am thoroughly poisoned, and no amount of
endless Parisian beauty can resurrect me to the stand-up station.

There was a six-feet man delete with a single silver argent starre.
He cast a long black shadow, high-heeled, & unfortunately, it was me.

O Tammy, I am but a fake *prince*, no horse, I stride all tall alone.
Only the demons come to me at dawn and say in unison: you'll be bonny once
again one day.

Delete the brightbairn, the laughing lad, the happy son, the singer of songs,
the larker out-larking the breast-high larks, out in the mad spring meadow.

Delete being under the hellhounds' paws, padding over thee,
right on your chestbreast, think yourself an upright man do you?

I've always believed I stood on the earth blessed with angel wings.
Even when I slurred terribly, mad with drink, my tongue was straight.

Delete fast pastures, hound hound alone with the pack,
hound with his vixen, and the endless need to attack.

Angel hound wings, hellhound hymns, no matter how many, no matter how
many, no matter how many, I will never like Sexton row to God,
I am alone with the pack on the frozen bypass without a wincing jade.

Houndangel wings, out of the sunne, and into northern starres,
hanging up your axe most prettily, O Em don't tongue-flay me!

Enemies say starchy but I say crispness & always tell the absolute.
You'll hide in my armlock, gently, for I am a passion prince.

Passion has always been me, even before my swollen drunken days.

Raw and savage and notwithstanding passion, all of me, all, all,
swanne on the misty lake to the very end of my days. Dark, willing

on my starre charger, high on the law, up on the fell, hear that
very single solo bell, by a fastly moving running river and under a completely
useless rainbow.

Anne Sexton Blues

I

Woke up this morning
        in Newcastle Wyoming
Atlanta Northumberland
on the glory grain plateaux of Texas
Anne Sexton all around my bed.

Honeyfix thighbone lustmoan, she said,
        you're not dead.
you're just mixing your breath with mine.
Vodka on or off the rocks, and wine.

Fierce delight possessed us while sober
        and mischief of a puckish strain: we were alone
in the blues rain in the banjo snow
in the cold blow of the Smirnoff
and the Black Label.
We stood within each other on the porch
and encouraged the magnolias to explain.

She put her gluey lips to mine, absolutely,
        lipstick and vine,
someone grieving kissing a person
about to be dead in Tumble Down Town.
        Her not me.
A Catholic priest in her passion.

I know you're riding there,
        she said, country boy bred
to Tyneside Texas: all the moths flying
around the light in our head.

Hands palmed, each side
of the upturned face:
man nails on man's hands;
woman nails on woman hands.

Woke up this morning in bad Feral County.
Anne Sexton's detoxing palms all around my bluesy
broken
        and banged down head,
Alamo heart burned and betrayed,

mixing her breath with mine.

II

The smart of my heart over you
flows like levee water all over my scripts
and streams and wishes and dreams.

It begins to rain in the pepper groves
but will not drown in the storm drains
the strains of my George Jones dreams.

Learn, fix-it-head, cries the high lonesome
sound,
        learn Mr Maniac Blues
it swifts through the jacaranda trees, head
down to be educated O escape motif organiser,

it is time you bridled up and went, to go:

Horror damage consultant,
                  heart bomb lover,
flick of the wrist terrorist,
                      Mr Big Bang Fascinated,
drek tongue class act in the shadow of the mesa cast
by the lonely song you bring.

Fake casuals lack the urgency
I need to search all scorchings:
may their lethargy never cease.

Peace is a requiem without flowers
and now we're completely at war.
Funny things happen: you – me.

Feast upon this brotherhood
of spanner menders, smarm monkeys,
cross lingerers, stone rollers, fancy
Dans and O'Hara babes:

Here on the busted bottle porch and stairs
there is only one sunne to ride into
to smash our ever driven apology

for sleep to smithereens.

Your Love Is A Swarm And An Unbeguiled Swanne

So there you are lying down here breasts
                    abreast in the argent dawn
and I lust after you and love you.
The devil or the devil's disciple's
                    will not take my sucking lips.
He will not, will not, have thee: I will. I will put them with my lips
and your lips,
and they will meet and furnace the night and dawnlight
in Miltonic chill and heat
all fingers pointing.

There is something to real love indescribable.

Standing on a January morning hunched together on a gatepost
when snow starts
is like I hope heaven will be.
                    Faces just touching.
There is something about just touching
which is touching
beneath the start of morning birdsong, when peewits take off,
breaking from cover
and the musick of the becks and burns appear louder,
miles away from traffic,
and the sonata of the clopping of beasts through clarts.

There is a lightness
in this almost dark, snow brightening the fields, hardening the ground,
when fingers smoothly, keenly, without damage,
cause fantastic sensations within the people involved.

Damp moss on the palms of the hands.
Wet stile steps
and the slippery burn bridge. Careful now.

Winter hard thistle prick a real joy.

More snow and it's colder
but our hearts and minds are hotter
than ever before.

A dawn of many beings and things.

Strap Down In Snowville

O hello, Othello, black and green bastardo,
please be Mr Stepaside. I've arrived.
It is dark now and always dark.
And demons will step from that darkness.
I am the Pookah Swanne MacSweeney,
wingflap homme man, jalousie
my daily trade – my eternal war game
against you and the world, drunken to the last, flung
to the lost in the final Labour council-run
public toilet on earth.

All moons waned and keeled, peeled
of sanity and treasure of esteem,
lollbonce on black plastic rim,
bottle of Hennessy and a Football Pink,
's'all I need, unbuckled pants ankle-dropped,
now that the greenwood
is stacked for fire, and me the inebriate sodden slave, tree
destroyed by a legion of governments
and the studied stupidity
of the lapsed intelligence of the people of England.

It is dark now along the river and always dark
where we rievers and berserkers have our mad seizure way.
Who needs life, when you're sucking France's finest
and all the infogen necessary for amour of a breezy future
without ballooning liver count is strictly in the Pink?

Who here needs a bardic throne on Christmas Eve
in the tiled cubicle of magic marker messages – Proper
Gay Sucks: Ring this number. No Jokers Please?
's' all the reading I need before Harvey the Rabbit
arrives pushing his white fur balls in my swollen
face and the armies of rock-steady Goliath ants
in bent Durrutti Columns proceed righteous
from urinal drain under bolted door of this cuboid
cubicle paradise hell, up the wall and into my eyes.

It is dark now along my swan meadow river and always dark.
The shutters at Boots are coming down for Christmas
and my last chance to get better is going with the closing
of the electric tills.

We did not burn enough magistrates' houses. We executed
one king but did not drag out enough Tories, and hang them
from the greenwood tree.
These forever here in the snow-laden urinal are my hysterical
historical regrets. Swan Lud, get my poster, did you?

Freed from cognac bondage on anti-spasm Dr Dolittle
sweeties I'm Swan as I like under Elvet, wings awry
to bust a neck for once not quite my own in bent back
guzzle down fast mode.

                    I DIE HARD, Pookah Swoony
Sweeney Swan Ludlunatic, revelling Leveller without
sober reveilles to look for in the broken indices.
Your sleek torpedo cowgirl heels have gone again
and it is dark now along the weir and always dark.

You'll not return as long as I drink at fermented
dementing demesning streams. But I'm all set-up!
This is *my* toilet cubicle now! I can vomit as I like.

Clap hands, here come the tinselled demons now,
carolling away the broken night and broken angel me
myself I&I yours truly Bob's Your Auntie Mabel,
downed by cognacflak, Spitfire tailrudder flutter.
Bellyflop on Magwitch marshes, hollied demons
rise from methane mist in one Christmas cracker chorus:

Let's hear it for the fratchy fractured Geordie ploughboy
playboy, collapsed and weeping in his bent furrow.

Let's fix a bright planet from a parallel universe
unto his dead starre skyless recovery agenda.

Let's leave him in the auburn pools of piss in his
frozen kingdom cubicle with Santa's reindeers revved.

Let's poke out his kindly eyes of purest borage blue
so as not to shirk a Guernsey tomato face lying deep
in the frozen lake of the mirror.

Let's not brush but switch & broom his quivering
lids with tail feathers of garrotted larks, pollen of larkspur,

let's elect him chief celebrant and Mr Big Advisor
at the amazing red ant hoolie; aconite posies in his rotten head.

Let's book him into the spineyellow pages of forgetfulness,
under Giant Guzzle Unlimited Forever & White Knuckle Rides

To Nowhere Fast – Spectacular Passing Out Our Speciality.
Let's hit the digit snap arrival button so he cannot wipe the sick away.

Let's for auld lang syne and weird kindness' sake, hush our
bee-sting lips with fingers upright, tiptoe in the snow we go
and leave the slurry-loving, slurry sleeping lad alone.

Stripes on your shoulders, stripes on your back & on your hands.
Strips & stripes & little books & daddy's tearing flaring point of view.
Like it son, or cry bruised and fearing for the rest of your solemn.

Solo days away from the palace of portion plenty & peace. Exeunt smiles.
Snow on my forehead, snow in the lock. Snowfall tick-tock slowly
winding downwind arms adrift inside it like a clock.

Demons tongue-stalking, mouth-walking: they're talking
              East Berlin, talking Grunewald, looking
              at their Dalí watches on stiff drink wrists.
Crazy in capitals, dark star ferment: no thee at the go place.

Clap hands, here they come. Clapped bellhead, angel boyhood
to scarred bottledom, British West Hartlepool to Benidorm.
Snowblindness cover me, smother my waxy wiggle tongue.
Snow blow me. All the snow-wind's a berserk bugle
here in my closet kingdom on the rim of mad Noel.

Sober up tomorrow, clean shirt, shakefinger tieknot,
well-ironed, iron the drink out of my face, unbolt my self:
avoiding the Lost Chance Saloon in favour of Maybe
One More Choice To Make in the Department Store of Sighs.
Pick up a bargain, stride home with purpose through
the jigsaw snow and the ghost of all demon daddies
to sit feet up and watch It's A Wonderful Life on the telly.
Oh, yes. Certainly. No fulminations or bare excuses.
Yours soberly your favourite son miserable ever after.

Sweeno, Sweeno

Sweeno is two people – at least. Sweeno the night crawling homme man,
soaked sapien, gutter treasurer & curled up counter of cobblestones

in twitch vision. Nightjar Sweeno – bliss buster supremo Sweeno.
Sweeno the long cry rising like missile fins from the fans' end.

Eyeless child blind on the grim uphill road to courthouse
compensation claims and the blindness of eternal non-recovery.

Sweeno lathed and lathered with port-soaked Baudelaire gingercake
alone as nitrates usher from the gargoyle's twisted seizure face.

It is hundreds of feet in the air but it is a black mirror of Sweeno's
collapsed kitten lover's pansypetal printwheel pout. Swooney

Sweeno's beano, born on a booze cruise, Sweeno at the entrance marked
Out. Go go Sweeno the demons said as they dunked his fairy brain

and fried his head. Earn your bread like Barrymore before
you're dead, trashed the tuneful trolls in unparalleled register

& roguish misdemeanour. That's showbiz, Sweeno, you drunk Dan Leno.
Between foot and wing, Sweeno learned one vital thing: You cannot

be wolf or stag alone in taiga treeline forever, peltcrested
& snowhorned, harpstrung highly-strung up Swoonatic,

haunt of hard-nosed hornets underneath your bonny steelbonnet.
Learn early skinstrip and sell it by the rotten mile. Learn unsmile.

Sweeno the Olympian champ diver down 20 stairs half an inch
from a broken neck. Seaweed Sweeno the man on the rocks a wreck.

Yet there's another side to Sweeno, the man with eyes of borage blue,
the man high up in the heather hills with his Grace Darling, plover's

wingbeat driving his brain and snipe drums beating his heart.
The upright Sweeno whose streaming becks are a life's fuel. This

is not King Fool, prisoner in toilets armed with caustic cognac,
this is the prince of the northern air, with his tough tender love.

Feldspar finder, tickler of wild brown trout, bridger of burns,
man alive in love his heart in the skyblue sky, o heather o, Sweeno!

But really the truth is less poetic and palatable. This is the acid
bath boy, the angel with hissing meat right off the bone. Strong

tongued with viper juice, bamboo snake in jungle of his own
green many-fingered making. Mocker and mucker-up of true

love which dwells in a strong house. In perverse poise and perfect pose
he draws upon cynical strength of four Betty winds to see it down

into the grinding tumblestone quartz which splinters and thrills
in atomic smash-up as the devil grins inside his skull tornado.

This is the big riff: look out, look out, but don't beware for
you cannot step aside. Sweeno's black guitar's on fire in

the human cathedrals of sense. The strings used for garrotting
moths before fireflames can ever reach their secret wing dust.

Sweeno the freak born a year early 1947 and kept for questioning
in Area 51. Then Sweeno's far-out mind went underground into

every ravaged corner he could find that no one else had touched.
Window-eyed and shutters down, fury festered in his fists

that execution plans for kings and queens and Tories had been
shelved. Greenwood tree over his stupid centuries skeletoned

into failed jigsaw of parched twigs and boughs. Failed opportunity
flailed his heart, Sweeno sick and resentful as brighteous righteous sin.

Yonder stalk the trance monsters dancing through the dark
distressing dew at dawn, demons holding babies, Sweeno's

Siobhan, leaving them upon the cold and open heartless
ground alive in itching gravel and grass with Betty blasts

of four winds to the heart. Sweeno's queeno in weep mode
when the ox-bow river of beauty busts its bushy banks

and all the riveted bridges Sweeno built can turn to mere rust.
Sweeno lying Lazarus in reverse on sick bed singing sickly:

Come down fleet rain and rinse my filthy dirty Betty soul.
Marry me to the chainlink fencing which like wild roses

extend their pricky pushy Jesus crowns into my vowbox bullet
tongue until strangled I&I like realo Sweeno me-o shall never rise again.

Sweeno sweating in the night, feeling the demon daddies his
flimflam framboise on ice cutting crew quiz his seizure bouncing

bedhead bonce raising the ratroof of his profane wordpush pillswallow
dickhead announcement zone, rawling on brain's hardbone basilica:

I AM THE NIGHTMARE. The blue tattoo legend bound to your Betty
sick soul forever. Kill that wasp. Beat it to death. O daddy demons, pin

its marigold and charcoal waistcoat stripes onto my Sweeno earholes,
lace together all its stricken wings for spectacles so I may read

again the many words of shattered vows, now I hear them struggle
into a storm of syntax once more as deadly distances which get

longer rise as steam from swamps here in the death-enclosing
night. No more for me the rising of a pink punk sun, black's

the colourway for Sweeno the Uncleano this very very day.
All separations yes, haul them in in blood-scrubbed bucketloads.

Fragments and distressed alphabets or arithmetic of misery
bound in distrust thrusts of gruesome guise laughingly we call

honour friendship and the universe. No rules now no greenwood
tree. The guillotines sent to Paris and none so near Sweeno's

hover handle hands. Not enough Ludlunatic posters pinned.
O please, Messrs Demon and Sons, vintage vintners and plyers

of slurtalk trade, pour Sweeno just one more before the heart
fails to grow and goes. Hear meano Sweeno: See what they did

to Elvis. Delilah haircut meets loss of power. Demon drink-up
death dribbles, absolutely, do take notes. No Samson Victor Manure

pillar push-downs. No push-ups but freely as the vomit streams
yanked by demon digits belly to basin. One day choke on it, tongue

jammed backward down throat's clogged highway. No noose good
news for those old escaping Tories. Enclosed meadows and one

executed king. Dreams so fierce, desert storms of ABC, all
fall down. One head enough. Not enough work done. Sweeno's

thin historical hysterical schedule in a spin. Sweeno in a mean
lean-to for Hurricane Betty: I've seen one hundred hungry dogs

crawl across their loved ones. I saw the skin fall from me
in steady strips and felt the sandpaper of so-called love

in eye of the very bone storm. I heard the wind say: I'm
blowing a mad and magic mojo horn and in the whipsong

of its Betty burned-out beauty – you call it filthy hatred and
betrayal for sad and solo Sweeno you are truly and completely

insane-o – I heard faintly from across the mountains far:
I'm going to lay down a thousand spells upon this unholy

disavowed ground until each writhing wily smiley wizard
downs his divining rods and realises finally at last at least

that they face a mixed trip back to Demon Town, and that
Demon Town is dead and Sweeno too will walk the line.

I'm afraid it is not possible, Sweeno in white strapjacket,
pilled to the nines, the nine winds, flung down the stairs

half inch from a noose-drop neckbreak in wake of Bettygate.
These are the lies, the footpad fingering falsehoods which

cannot nor will not, will not, will not, fall away rapidly
expiring. Falsehoods dark as my meadows are darkly dark

as the river and the roaring weir are dark & always dark.
When did you last see your father the insane interrogative

bells boomingly in his echoing bentneck at stairfoot as
another bottlebung pulled pop! right out and bolted down.

O chief stockholders in future equities of a rising thirst,
Sweeno is achieving major results in a shaky flaky market.

Sweeno cleans up and swallows down in dead of night
when others have gone home. He's a winning wino alright.

Don't doubt, deadly debt collectors all, look at the dividends
diving towards the rising expectations of a life in the sun

alliance, Sweeno's dalliance dance with death is legend now.
Sweeno's right there on the job. Pour him another and be grateful.

Anti-Lazarus Ludlunatic lolltongue Lollard, wine pourer
down his neck of night purrings, reports say Sweeno's

on the mend or round the bloody Beaujolais bend. Exit Rex.
No glory on the bottlefield overdrawn at the bottle bank.

Must have carpet experience. Presumably to roll king's
heads down the corridors of flexed power surge control.

The very trim, very slim experience of the twisted days;
days of yes I'm damned again and dimmed again by demons.

Days of bile man, slime man, vomit on his Texas shoes.
Glass glints purchase sunlight as birds and long-haul

planes fly through. Awful day, bad as any government.
Turkey plucker wanted – Norfolk. Head down the pan again.

What does it mean: to spew your ring? Sweeno, Sweeno,
you have vast experience of sickness – do you know, Sweeno?

No, no, no, hands up against any human requests at decency,
Sweeno's on his own-io, lone striker on his flat back four.

Ten years in the same team Going Nowhere Albion sponsored
not just match days Cellar 5, Victoria Wine, Threshers, Red

Wine Rovers, Plonk Park Disunited, The Old Dysfunctionals,
Soused Spartans, Inter Chianti's chanting demons' unflagging

fandom: Sweeno, Sweeno, give him a bottle he scores a goal.
Own goals mostly, catalogue of lost memory matches & scores.

Hands on knees and puffing hard I've had enough of this.
Ankle-tapping, broken bones, demonic shirt-pulling, the

beautiful game on the emerald field of dreams now turf
churned, filthy, white line I shimmy down impossible to see.

Chants, rants for Sweeno, zero hero. Come on ref, blow that whistle.
Rockets, fires and flags on trouble-free terraces. Ferocity

like mine. No-score draw. No extra time. No penalty shoot-out. No
golden-goal finale, no golden boot. Down the tunnel into nightlight. Endgame.

Up A Height And Raining

I

O just to vex me inside the bottle the wind stayed still,
and left correct my cheap Woolworth accoutrements.
Look at the sheep fleece from tumbler base, so finely
doused by rain from Garrigill, as I dance my demon tarantella
in the misty mire.

I stood on the hill with drenched face and soaking nerves,
ankle deep leaving the word sober at home, gobsmacked.
The upstream heather says more than I do, whispering
its purple blues.

I wanted it to blow tonight, to put it right,
to put my G-force twisted face back in place.

Brown leaves now on the beryl lawn

                                        and the magpies are gone.

The golden rowan an ascending beam.
Arctic white roses from the Himalayas
white as the whites of my eyes used to be
before the demons held my lapels.

It is dawn and soon I will have a fit,
a seizure, a gagthroat convulsion,
a demon convention with furtongue
pressed hard against the roof of my mouth.

Mouth an estuary for the love of drink,
and I know I stink of it darling
and no amount of mints or garlic can hide it
from the houndsniff now that's built into your mind.

There will be blood, dearest, and horrid venom,
and black demon matter we'll never clean off.
I won't go again onto the drip. Not to the hospital
or the lock-away ward with its tightly kept key.
I'm going solo with capsules and the strength of your love.

Yes, love, they come: shiny shoes oddly enough,
the very nature of poetry erased from their report books,
tight black leather gloves to grip the bottles. Those
ugly gloved hands which search your soul.
You must guzzle aloud and let them do it
for every demon has to have its day.

My silence endless except for the swallowing.

O look at the golden leaves retrieved from the pink-sleeved trees
by the very act of the earth and its seasons.
They are bronze and gold, how very precious and horizontal
they are this regal collapsed November.
Look how they fall from the trees, quite drunk
with an unknown dream of renewal.

No stopping them and no stopping me
parallel to the horizon: my licence laws very strict –
I go from glass to glass, bottle to offy and back.
There's one thing you can say: I never slack
from TV cornflake zone until Big Ben's a post epilogue memory.

Except I can't remember it or anything
unless the mind-piranhas begin to swarm
and I know I am not Cromwell or Milton
but I am a Protestant heretic,
a Leveller lunatic, filled and felled by wine,
whose failed allotment is a museum of weeds,
whose rainy medallions are mare's tail and crowsfoot trefoil.

I do remember a blue light turning, and turning
to you and trying to speak and couldn't. Just
the bleeps on the machine trying to keep me alive.

And after X-ray escaping the wheelchair, vodka-legged,
felled face down by the drink in the street.
Nervous pedestrians leaning over
and a discerning passer-by: leave him he's pissed.

II

Perhaps I will rise in the fronds of Bengal
        crushed and tormented but determined to live
fantastically luxurious in the grandness of suffering
        searching for the lingering lips of her loveliness:
today I hunted through the wide wild skies,
not one finger to touch, not one sunshine dalliance alliance.

Arm rodded cloudward, always wanting the lightning mine.
I wanted to be the driver on the Leningrad train, screeching
        raptor of the whole northern air: sober groom with a bride.
Beasts steam and clop by the wire where my bottle is hidden,
        secret menu for peace, rage and change.

III

Yes, alcoholic, get him out of my face.

Gin in his nose he's a Christmas reindeer
every day he won't keep in his diary.
Holy mother, free him from my terrorised tree.
Release him from the twines of the briar,
see him flash to the cork in fen and fern.
Collapse him in misery. Slap him away.
Give him 45 per cent voltage and watch him go.

I am Sweeney Furioso, fulled with hate.
Hate for you, for me, hate for the world.
I eat beasts nightly and chew on snakes.

The blood of an invented heaven spills from my shoes.
I rage with wrecked harp
                              for I am not the silence of Pearl
though she is inside me, like an argent moon.
I am a beast myself and return to see the mint die.
All that is left are drought-stricken stems.

There is no doctor cure.
There is no god and I believe it.
Every capsule in every brown bottle
is a pact of deceiving; the demons know.
Every prescription is a contract of lies.

I set my slurring lips against the stupid universe.
I squeeze my mouth as best I can around a bottleneck and mean it.
Daily I fix my redlight eyes against the raw law sunne
shaking my detox fists at the rams and lambs.
It will make me powerful if they flee from me.

Sorry is the last word in the long lost dictionary.
There was a man once, in a long thin box.
I see his washed out face in the fellside chapel.
We'll put out flowers and drink to his memory.
We'll scatter his ashes and drink some more.

The aim is victory over the sunne and to stand in a high place
holding a red flag
ready to lead unforgiven workers to righteous triumph.
You must execute kings and adulterous princes
and reserve the right to burn down Parliament.
Fight for your rights for the rest of your days.

IV

At Sparty Lea, here is the breeze burn,
at the bend in the bridge here is the stile squeak.
Here at the west window is the speaking for Pearl.

Here in the clouds is her eloquent silence
before addiction overwhelmed me and
made me silent myself. Her night cloud silence

following the clouds. And the clouds following
her and the light in her heart. She sails in
galleons of light all the way to Dunbar.

We seized the sky and made it ours, spelling
out the vapour trails: our clouds exclusively
before poetry was written, long before harm

and its broods of violence. Before we knew
the moon was cold and before men – real
men – stood upon it for the very first time.

But love, that moon, that moon is ours,
always, cold as your distant tongue.

V

Smoked salmon and lemon juice for breakfast,
  brilliantly chosen brewed teas!

The enticing slow lifting of garments, wearing
  and unwearing of black silk,

and exchanging of black and blue silks, white
lingerie chemise taken off as the mist rises
  to meet its handsome lover the sunne.

Underneath sheet lightning
      with audible thunder,
lightning down the rod and sceptre,
       kisses fuming in darkness,
electric discharge between clouds,
      fecund trenches & moss cracks.

Zig-zag bones and branching lines fully displayed,
                              diffused brightness to cooling toes
before unwinding unwounded stretches of sleep.
                              Kissed slumber barely awake
under the vast viaduct:
                              sex combs, complete claspness,
hairs locked and unlocked,
                              special pet favours given and received
on both sides.
                Defying gravity.

Our passion, darling, is pure 1917. We ride
                              the rods and rules and rails,
and skies for us will always be huge and authentic:
                              Northumberland Wyoming and Samarkand.

Fierce not the word to use for our kisses.
                              It is not fierce enough!
There are no wounds
                and revenge and warfare will die in the mud
of an otherwise poor world.

Fireflies, conductors, heads limbs and hearts,
                wires fixed to the great wide skies:

We diverted heaven's light
                into sea or earth's true bounty

of our souls' brilliant kisses and everlasting starres.

Tom In The Market Square Outside Boots

Tom you're walking up & down the pill hill again.
Tom you're taking your moustache
 to the Ayatollah doctor with his severe case
 of personality drought.
Tom I saw you in the Heart Foundation shop
buying a cardigan five sizes too big.
Tom you're more bent over than when
we sat together in the locked ward.
Tom your coat is frayed like the edges of your mind.
Tom they let you out to the chippy but you're not free.
 Tom we're falling in the wheat
our feet betrayed by sticks and stones.
 Tom we're in the laundry and it's us spinning
as they try to dry out our wet lettuce heads.
Tom there's a cloud on the broken horizon
 and it's a doctor with a puncture kit.
He's got a mind like a sewer and a heart like a chain.

Tom, who put the rat in the hat box?
Who gave the snakes up the wall such scaly definition?
Who plastered the universe with shreds of attempting?
Who unleashed the foes to annex your head?
 Who greased the wheels of the Assyrians' chariots?

Tom the shadows of men are out on the river tonight
                                        reeling and creeling.
 Invaders from Mars have arrived at last
  and they're working in the lock-up wards.
 They're dodgy Tom, strictly non-kosher – just raise your hangdog
 blitzed out brain and look in the defenestrated alleyways
      which pass for their eyes.
 I suspected something in the fingerprint room
 & the sniggery way they dismissed our nightmares.
 Tom the door is opened
                        and you lurch down the path
   past the parterre and the bragging begonias
 but listen Tom
              on the cat's whisker CB
                              listen Tom listen and look
  you're still a dog on a lead a fish on a hook

Tom you're a page in the book of life
 but you're not a book
  you're not the Collected Works of Tom – yet
there's no preface but the one they give you
   there is no afterword because no one knows you
   there's a photo on the cover but it doesn't bear looking at
    there's a hole where your family used to be
    an everlasting gap in the visitors' index
A SMILE FROM THE NURSES LIKE THE BLADE OF A KNIFE

   Tom – what happened to your wife?
   She used to visit – every Wednesday
   when buses were running before the cuts

   Now she's a lonely bell in a distant village
   sacked by the Government
   Mr and Mrs Statistics
                        and their gluey-faced children

   There's only one job on offer
   in the whole of Front Street
   delivering pizzas to the hard-up hungry

      and a spanking new sign on the unused chapel
      Carpenter Wants Joiners
   Jesus Tom it isn't a joke
      they crucified the miners
      with Pharisees and cavalry
      dressed up as friendly coppergrams
      it wasn't Dixon of Dock Green Tom
      it was the Duke of Cumberland and Lord Londonderry
rolled into one

      Dark today Tom and the city roofs argent with rain
      dark as a twisted heart Tom
      dark as a government without soul
      or responsible regard for its citizens

   trains' rolling thunder north and south over the great redbrick viaduct
   is the only sense of freedom I have today Tom
   the high lonesome sound of the wheels on the track
   like Hank Williams Tom we'll travel too far and never come back
   which is why they drug us to a stop Tom
   pillfingers over our fipples and flute holes
   we're in a human zoo Tom and it's a cruel place

Tom you're away from a haunt but furled in a toil
Tom there's a spoil heap in every village without a colliery
 there's a gorse bush on top you can hide in naked
but you can't escape the molten golden rays of the sky
bleaching the leukemia lonnens of ICI Bone Marrow City
Tom out here on the A19 the long September shadows of England
stretch from Wingate all the way to Station Town
long and strong and dark as the heart of the Jesus Christ Almighty
or the lash of the snakeskin whip he holds over us all

Tom are you mad by north-north-west
                    or do you know a hawk from a handsaw?
 Are your breezes southerly?
All the fresh air is quite invalid Tom and all the peeping spirits
have ascended to your brain
                              like region kites
and the gall of the world is mixed in a cup

Tom there's a silent flywheel on every horizon sequestered by law
                                              & severed from use

   O dear, Tom, our heels are kicking at the heavens
   sulphured eyebrows as we strike into the hazard universe of souls
   where angels on our shoulders stand tall to make assay
   for acid rain will fall and wash them white as snow
   the weather has turned Turk Tom and we are almost ruined
    all softly cooling bright Atlantic winds from Cork and Donegal
   are cancelled now
   and fever has us in its grippy flame
   ill-fit saddles have galled our wincing jades
             all that is left is the mousetrap of the devil
    but only if you give up on humans

     Tom invisible limers are fingering twigs in the groves
     Tom the twin sears of my hammered heart are set to be tickled
                      by leather-sleeved index fingers itchy and raw
     Tom there's a man in black with a lone silver star
      casting a shadow as long as his dreams

     Are your eyelids wagging Tom, so far from the burning zone?
     Have they fitted you out yet, did you have the bottle to object?
     Tom I can see you being folded like a linen tablecloth
      I can see the busy working hands working on you

We've been driven from the prairies Tom
                   to an isthmus of disappointment
                             whose pinched becks can never sustain us

Tom I frighted my friends
                             by getting this way
                             I sickled and scythed their garlands of wheat
tongue a runaway bogie with broken brakes
alone on the pavings written with rain I was a sacked village myself
palings downed and all fat fields returned to pitiful scrub
                             Station Town Quebec Shincliffe to No Place

                   a network of underground ghosts
                   bust at the seams

Tom will our dear decorated hangers be responsive to the hilts on the swords
                                                  of our days?
          Will a tigerish revival leap upon us
                             from a leaf-locked lair?
          Will we be allowed another trample through mud?
          Tom I doubt it as the sunne doubts the starres.
          But starrelight is our single fire Tom, single
          and silver in the bed of the sky.

Brown-bottled venom and its work
                             a past prescription be
and all folded warriors
                             to gentle station grow.

The glow-worm dims and the sea's pearled crashy phosphorescence
in matin mist.

          There's a lark aloft in the morning Tom
                             its breasty song our autograph
          embracing fortune
                             in this out of focus world

                   high and mighty

                             and carried away on shields.

John Bunyan To Johnny Rotten

The long shadows of gold October stamped into the earth of England.
Amber crowns of trees shredded in the wake of the wind
whose invisible straps unwind allowing previously strapped grasses to become
unfleeced in air and have echoes and tunes like chapel hymns along the arm of
the law.
It is our rim of the world. It is our Aztec finality and birds fly there.
They are funny birds and bonny with aquamarine flashes down their pillowsoft
beakbone nearness & not like peewits at all.
It is our raining night & hoofing the wet lonnen. We are tearing down posters
at Loaning Head
pinned with one nail
and on the posters badly-drawn faces
for we are grey ghosts and silver surfers
the Finnbars the MacSweeneys the Pookas the Toms
the gun-carrying leadmineshaft knockabout nobodies
swimming beer off Sundays in the ice-cold tarn
never knocked down in Knock Down Town.
Nothing left in England now.
One king only not enough.
When did you last see your father is a laugh for me Tom, he was a jellied-eel traitor
to my poetic revolutionary heart
for always I have the axe in my hand. 1917. I have the hood and the axe and the
unsmilingness. I will do it as duty Tom, for waste must be punished.
O Tom, what am I saying?
I have wept before the shoals of shoes from Amsterdam, from Vienna, from
Warsaw, the leather straps and rusted buckles,
I wept before the Jewish mountain of shoes and sandals and encasements
purposefully stitched and modelled for feet whose feet-bringers were hoyed
in the ovens and the gas.
My axe alone Tom is against the oppressor & oppressors.
Tom, I'm not a poker-hearted Pooka. In sober raindawn reality I'm a cress-
hearted man.
No Caroline Louise no Hazel the pills are wearing off
I walk alive alone in Alston and lean against the menu of the Bluebell Inn
because it *is* mine. Smoke from the little trains are the fumes in my brain.
I walk there Tom, I run there Pearl. Rings to be made and vows to be said.
Tom, you have rockfire. Tom you have a lordly head.
Tom, can you hear the final slowing down spin of the flywheel
as the last cage ascends?
Tom, these are real men with faces like pandas
carrying badgerbrocks of coal. It's a memento now.
This place, Tom, *was* a nation, making trains and ships and cranes,

transporting unlikeables like us to the lands of boomerangs and redrock. Our
chainbroken fingers & hands acquainted with hunger & slavering slavery
kept together the hulks on the Thames, we were the true breath of the
nightforest noosehang land.
Tom, do you remember when lightly but enough to hear I knocked for you at
midnight, starres our only light, if starres there were? God help us Tom
we enjoyed it, one more Tory burned from his bed.
We stood together with tightly-bridled panting steeds among pooked sheaves
laughing until the sunne of togetherness warmed our roof-burning brand-
throwing shoulders.
How strong it was Tom, our amusement, as the red-coated militia arrived,
long before they drove down the miners in the villages. We blessed Jesus
the first Chartist for saving the bairns and the wife.
But the port-soaked Tory was dead, Tom,
and we sang our hymns with clean hearts.
Tom, nothing has changed except everything.

All of these centuries and centurions.
Tom, last night Milton & Cromwell said I should speak to you.
Bunyan smuggled a note on ragged paper.
Five knocks on the water pipe, I knew it was coming.
Tom, now it's us in the lock-up, in the spotty-face bathroom, in the lost
toothpaste universe,
in the argumentative wild Pearl honeysuckle wold unyielding unwielded world
of wrong-sized slippers, in the bad dressing-gowns
before harried relatives arrive to pull the armpits right, Tom, it's us: the walking
sandbaghead wounded dead of poor lost England.

I met Cromwell & Milton & Blake yesterday and they were lost as us,
funny stout men and one blind looking for the dreams of Albion.
Pen-ready men with quill of swanne.

Tom, you put your right shoe on your right foot and the left on the left.
The laces need to be tied and in absence of your apple-pie wife I'll do it
because bending down with firm fingers is so difficult
as pills plasticine your once-digitally correct hands and take the few straight
lines in your messed-up mind
and turn them into undriveable curves.

Even Blind Willie Milton even Cromwell even the Memphis Flash even
The Killer even Cash
is on a midnight Vincent Black Shadow.
From Huddie Ledbetter to de Kooning they're in slave overalls.
There's a pride in working for a living Tom, but it isn't for us. We're wasted
in wastelands before they were invented by Thomas Stearns Eliot.

Before Sylvia Plath paid her gas bill,
before Anne Sexton demanded blue disks from the doktor, before she
admitted an addiction to slavery & left us to be a spirit in the rainy trees.
Tom, King Arthur's in his counting house, counting out the wastage,
finalising the blame,
And who would say it, Thomas, who would lift the gall from the cracked glass,
but to say: Arthur, you too were a croupier of blame, you too
swept the table clean with the other social model, Margaret of St Francis?

Tom I do miss your wife Alice because for one reason at least
she brought us cloudy pastry tarts filled with apples from your trees
and sweetened by sugar from the Co-op in Langley Park
eating moon slices before pills travelled us to sleep
and Alice left sprightly rightly perhaps a purposeful heart searching for sunshine
in the darkness of day. Heart a mixed posse of love and not love,
of drawn guns and pouched bullets.

And a hatred of the Stasi experiment doktors shared by us all.

Tom, I want to lock the lunar lunatic's opal horns, I want to run before
the moon, I want to swing on my starres by Bunting, garlanded with squat,
I want to drink endless my Castrol to stop the stile squeak.
Tom, she's a princess of the mosswalks, and she does not want you to leave
her alone. And the bairns are crying for their dad, dad, lost dad, man with
moustache & a bone in his head.
Hard as a Birmingham spanner and right as a River Tyne rivet.
We're walking to the gay liberation centre, Tom, but we're already dead.

Taxi, Tom, heartsore, we're a pack Tom, infesting the age, thousands of thorns,
which may as well be pennies, someone to pay for it,
trainers for the bairns who know you're a photo once in the Sundays *borsik* in
the madman's paradise:
the club, Tom, the full-sized snooker table, where you can write in big chalk and
lay a fat man down: Tom, dear garlanded friend Tom, you're not that strong.

And if anyone picked on you, they'd have to peck at my fiststance darkdance first,
burst from the feldspar heifer hoof fields.
I am Lenz, underground my natural home. Watch me, Tom,
bust from the cowslip shadow alone with Pearl.

My heart and anger a double-barrelled sawn-off gun. Axe on hold whipped
clean by the wind from Pearl's mouth.
When did you last see your father, Tom can you help me?
Invisible he was forever when I was seven-years-old.
My canvas was clean but on it he put troubled colour.
Tom, the point is: I want that portion of him executed.

I know these hills so rest in my shadow.
I'll talk to the jailer and tea at dawn will be the leastest.
3764 Highway 51 South, Robert already having PASSED BY TO TOES
TURNED-UP TIME.
SURLY STEEL, BOLD STEEL, TUNNELS THROUGH ENGLAND,
TOM YOUR MIND'S LIKE MINE: PEASE PUDDING.
We're Navvies Tom. Straight up. Garlanded by bows of greenwood tree
and poem and lock-up ward and pill.

We are singing Milton today dreaming of Jerusalem
and the trains which never take us along the steel of the world.
Law with the wind in my face as I mince springingly princingly
on my wincing jade,
bit-jaw strapped in, fist-firm, fury in my heel spur and black frock coat
which can only bring death to the demons and the kings of frippery of England:

Law on the horizon and law in the lonnen at Loaning Head:
Stirrup-high I turn for the smell on the heather fellwind, still
on my mount, still but nostril light, honey of her thighs on Irish winds
before we gathered at night, building obelisks to Chartists
and we stroked goodnight the muzzles of upland high-hooved horses
because they reminded us of women lost in the dawn of the dew and dandelions

Tom I think I've gone turnip tuneless toes turned up frozen out from river
to rawness
on the rim of the law and the world
Tom a man came in a long black suit to saw off one of my limbs
before anaesthetic
Tom I pulled from my leather pouch – hole in its hiplength spout – a gun
with hammer of the finest steel, a curved knuckle-guard you'd wish to tell
your children about
if you lived beyond the rapes of the government

and Tom he didn't get any further
to you for example Tom because your brain's an oversteamed cauliflower
lolling in the Locomotive Arms
and my lover Tom my lover the poet is not a loader of rifles
a washer of signal cloths
she's a leader Tom she's a high-stepping jade herself
not one quick finger far from the pin

Tom, Pearl, I'm wedded to a theory from which I shall no doubt be soon divorced
in undainty circumstances
that disobedience
Disobedience, disavowal, the shredding of woofs and weaves,
the salivating of microphones
when all is denied, Bold steel low lot lacklevel.

I am these men and their lost women.
I am, spur-horsed, undenizened

Invisible twine plying merchants are unravelling the long grasses
and the plovering pull of the long windstrewngrasses pluck the prince
in his chest his heart his passion and love as if no tomorrow.

He caws, crows quietly, softly as a byre when beasts have departed
and rain on a shifted slate is like indescribable music which is
not music because the word is yet to be invented under the great heaven.
Let's wait for the very day Pearl says it whipped by rain. Beautiful Pearl.
And the leaves in the trees seem to whisper Louise because they're nuts Tom.

But I sank shaftshining in her budding cressbed. She's as wet as a 17-year-old.
They should be saying Michael Collins Bobby Sands and a litany a directory
in the wind from Sligo a stooked sheaf of telegrams of the dead the foolish
the aimless the aimed at the fallen and the framed Tom.
But they're not they're frozen like my angel in the fantastic magnet filings
of her boldly stirred heart.

So this is where you were in the he-boat the she-boat the he-she boast-come
together lover on the lake where the swans come in.
This is where the matin mount of your kisses wrestled with the oar-lock movings
for supremacy in the long mornings when the boat drifted into the reedbanks
This is where you rowed the he-boat and swam in the clear Irish water
and lay in his swanwings in the uncloaked unlocked dawn of padding
across the water
abandoned abandoned on the ferry landings of Ireland
pipes laid by for *Marie's Wedding* and *She Moved Through the Fair*
this is where my heart was a black kesh by the forlorn waves of the clear water
where the swans come
my heart my wooing MacSwooning whistling heart love
nothing but a black kesh in charcoal shadow on a sunless hill
I was a monster in Munster swinging my green jealous sword and making you pay

There were no telegrams Michael no messages Tom no letters the Royal Mail
is dead today but a bullet in the head and an army led by Judas
I do not believe him a good man

Soldiers need paying but he was not a soldier for freedom
only my heart will fight for her love and want nothing in return
but a kiss like a flutesong a hug like a tressed harp
a fire in her eyes and a dance in her hair
Tom there will be applause from the gatherings for the pressing and raising of heels
but it won't be for us
locked in the byre with the beasts and the winding gatepushing wind

Tom you know there'll be a wind from the west
all my life I've been a leader and now like you it's a lost soul department
nothing to say Tom but this poem
& the rare beautiful women of Doncaster beneath the High Street clock
Tom rarely sick
                    garlanded by sullen steel
Tom in the tunnel with the dynamite mob
and the jelly in his drainbrain
& mine
its gutters and flues of intelligence flowing away to a land filled with fairies

where Tom

rarely sick and rarely better
                         threw doll from his pram
on gallery 10
where the screw was hanged with piano wire

we dawdled in the bronze-leaved sullen golden sleeves of the sike paths
threads of earth in the matin mist above the toy cathedral
edgewater clouded with invisible natural matter the human eye will never see
so you say for something to define it the water is clear to the bottom
pebble gatherings clear as the tumbler base seen through gin and vodka
brought by demons from the piggery where my heart lay in ruins
as now it lies ruined Tom
altogether Minister of Mayhem to Myself the great bombardier the single swanne

for she is swooning for his harpstrum lips all the way from the ferry landings
to the grid systems of New York and the sunsets of boulevards Tom
we shall never know with our bed end hangdog
broken busted barely visible beatitude
waiting the bolt to the temple
we're in a byre Tom it's true
                         and the transience of love hammers us all

and no swan call no flashing nuthatch

no rain on the gravel or mist in the hair
can save us from the eternal prospekt of the knacker's yard

red berries on the holly bushes Tom but we'll never see Christmas
there'll only be wreaths
not paid for by plastic
we'll never see Christmas

except with the angels

                    pulling us towards the argent arcs of starres
elegies unwritten left for those alive below

to argue and fuss over lost blood bones and brains

<u>!GOD SAVE THE</u>

<u>QUEEN!</u>

UNCOLLECTED POEMS

[1983/1997-1998]

La Rage

(for Lesley)

Irish poets
call it *rhosin dhu*
but I call it
la rage.
The black rose rage
that argibargies
your heart.

Magic is la rage.
The shaman
knows la rage.
The throws
of the runes
& sticks
& stones,
the terrible tunes
& the terrible truth
of the scattered bones
are la rage.

The root of the word
for lemon and bird
and curlew and curd
is la rage.

When the French
get la rage
they sit
sur la plage
and watch la mer
go spare
with liquid
la rage.

Oompah oompah
stick it up your junta
I want to gorge
like Billy Bunter
because I've got
la rage.

I want to zoom across
your harbour
singing tora tora tora
then send you
bunches of love in a mist
via interflora
because I've got
la rage.

Chaucer calls it
mercyless beautie
Little Richard calls it
tutti frutti

Bill Haley calls it
Rock Around the Clock
and Elvis calls it
Jailhouse Rock

but to me it's just
la rage.

And Shakespeare
whose vocabulary
is much larger
calls it
something else

but the arrow flies
like William Tell's
to the apple
of your eyes

because you have
la rage

That strange ancient sting
abracadabra
makes me want to swing
like Errol Flynn
from any old candlebra.

I want to buckle
and swash
have a chuckle
and talk posh
steal Phyllis Marlowe's
double-breasted
raincoat cosh

because I've got
la rage.

I want to wipe
pistachio
from my ripe
moustachio
and tinkle
ivories
till dawn.

When champagne
flows
we'll go
and go
and draw
the curtains
when a star
is born.

When Ravi
Shankar
plays that
raga
I want to
bathe
in Holsten
lager

because I've got
la rage.

I want to ruin
Anello & Davide shoes
walking on peat bogs
with you.

Let's put on
our Sunday suits
raid the love bank
steal the loot

because we've got
LA RAGE.

1983

Don't Leave Me
(for SJL)

Underneath the western starres, my heart is sore

      & bruised. Soft rain on the elderflowers' creamy upturned ladles.
You speak at me in silence like a lightning strike.

No bells chiming, but it is midnight of the soule.
Don't leave me in this empty world without you.
      Dear postmistress, kick the tilth right in my face,
wear longingly lovely charcoal black lace, fan into
the room like a silk torpedo, hang from the rafters
like a bird. Imitate an irritated bat from hell. But
please succumb to the final mad announcement:
Don't leave me in this lonely world without you.

The great sunne dies, the argent moon strides
along its Pearly path. Our hearts and minds and
mouths fume and fix in a terrible acid bath. It
is awesome the way we meet and fight for love.
But fight we must – ring that bell, ring that bell.
Once aloft in heaven's light, now in scarlet hell.
Don't leave me in this lonely world without you.
Coinage of the word trust debased beyond belief,
all that's left remaining is a broken whitebeam leaf.
Unique information on the history of solar winds
enters the busy avenues of the hive of my heart;
O yes the kestrel's wings are not as lonely as me:
the argent dreamstreams, the places we undressed.
Clouds like crowns above the merry nodding cranesbill.
See the leadmine workings above the hill and the beck –
O Pearl, life has its middensmitten mittens around my neck.
She has signed a contract with relentless punishment.
Inside the rim of the silver ring I always wear its legend says:
Don't leave me in this lonely empty world without thee.
I blink aloft for once at the total madness, hawkeye,
listening to your scorn in the harsh proving grounds.
This is government truly dark, don't believe the headlines
so freakish glandular. Beneath the rainy viaduct I stand
well-pressed fully-bagged and weep alone for want for want
of you. Stupidly I worry about your lack of extra virgin olive oil.
Your chest, my chest. You'd think I was a strutting Nazi
with an acorn crest. What's lost is probably best, but please
don't leave me in this viciously stupid world without you.

I need your elbows in my ribs, I need your snores. I need
to make you tea as the magpies puffbelly the hospital hill.
I need your attentive attention at my continual pills and sores.
Now that the workmen are sandblasting our Malevich bridge
and I am not a one-night bum from the halls of hell I can only
say please don't leave me in this loveless world without you.

She came wet-haired O delete her fargone farflung lips!
There was a cranny there was a niche there was a feather.
There was the most important date in history it was 1966.
I alone singular bombed Coventry she would not spare me.
Who am I at last, the final One Eyed Jack? Ace heart man.
She came fret-laired, rivet-lipped. I flew a Junkers 88.
And as the bombs threw up their little distant powder puffs
to which I had no allegiance in the night sky I said into the
intercom please don't leave me in this lonely world without you.
There was the most important date in history it was 1968 it
was the Citroën workers it was the Sorbonne it was cobblestones.
All the time assaulting policemen and being assaulted I was
looking for thee from dawn till dusk from start to finish I wrote
please don't desert me in this vile forsaken world without you.
Notebook entrance: here in Derbyshire in the high hills her
with the finest legs I glanced at. We were firmfurious together.
She had and has a line in language I love a lot. Fulled with abstracts.
Saw Blake saw Wallace Stevens saw no things but in ideas.
She had a poetry fullwritten and a beautiful face to match.
Monsieur Bleak, Black, Noir, Personne Spared, Homme Of The Moone.
Homme walking tall, homme particulier de l'alientation mentale.
I cannot walk this earth unless you take on board the message
that I cannot live in this unaccompanied vastness without thee.
I punch, I fist, I turn your faces around my wrist. My heartache
is a long river – there's a handled gunne & spangled fingernails
will see it drawn in horizontal spitfire. O love I love you
and I cannot live in this lonely world without you. The blitzblack
BirminghamCoventry merle sharpens its cornyellow on the shedend.
Except for us it is the mating time. Delicious peach at the start
of my life, don't leave me in this wildweed world without you.
The wild grass sings and the herb flowers under a frantic sky.
Chouchou flechette, j'arrive bien sur, alors je suis pliant, et tu:
Ne me quitte pas au univers solitaire sans tu. Je t'aime, je t'aime.
If your distress is not quite ready I have my own. Think of me
if you have time between Barnard Castle and Darlingtown. Turn
your loving heart in my terrible direction. Don't be cold impossible.
Don't leave me bleakblokefaced in this sad and lonely world
without you. I don't want my genocide peak to call the world Pauline.
Once more the grievance deep, larks&laughs killed despairingly;

once more the two doors opened for the demons: welcome, boys!
They are setting them right up at the bar in their midnight overcoats.
Darling, I am attracted by them, but I am more attracted to you.
Sweetheart, today the bullion sunshine rays down unshared.
DucktoedDoucement, peafinger, lapjuice, cannylass, stalkwalker,
the light begins to twinkle on the rocks. How right you are to hate me.
But please don't leave me in this lonely empty world without you.

Spit drooling down splashes on left wrist. I will detox now.
It will take two days and then I will be alright. Borage blue again.
Petal poet, soft as the very earthe, against all damned enclosures,
poetess, don't ever leave me in this hardened world without you.
The brazen sky is a hardened screwdriver. I will not bend. War
between ourselves, despite creamteas, you keep abandoning me.
Standing on the rained-upon steps we are reduced to verbal beggary,
flakes & tatters of verbs and adjectival despair. Only the tangerine
sage grows. I turn my back in hope it will not hurt, but all I want to
say is please don't leave me in this wet and lonely world without you.
My blood is high and I am fierce with love for you. It will not end.
I'll feed the information keys forever but it won't make a difference.
There is nothing between us now but the four o'clock starres.
O
they are making up a tattered sky as I walk the night and elsewhere
you sleep. Eel body. Slippy skin I can't catch you or have you in my net.
Don't blame me for Coventry, I was not even born; this is not you
middle-England, but harsh England, fatherly teatime headblows,
those of a kind which deafened Beethoven as a lad. Excuse this
cablegram: Don't leave me in this rotten filthy universe without you.
Monday, slumday is a wipeout. I palm away those thrusting beasts
in skinny pinstriped suits and badly-ironed shirts. Prettyboys
useless! Sleep with them Ireland and Germany one night only.
Darlingest, I want you for more than one night. Fells and streams.

Wild, wet, without conventional wisdom. 3.26 a.m. Beast in rain.
Me.

What kind of deformed chicken thighs are these?
What kind of very un-Irish potatoes we sailed off from?
to this sad and sorry land? Is that, my love, my deepest love,
why I love rain so much, because I was born beneath it?
We executed only one king. It was not enough. Please don't
please don't leave me in this lonely universe without you.
I lie beneath the greenwood tree and weep my very heart away.
Claw tthroat [correct], sink ticket, produit, elle est belle, tres.
Now it is a day of fallen cooking apples and reluctant mist,
webbed among the shaking limbs of the Williams pear tree;

& sage – thus flowered – and thyme, so brill blue, so fragrant,
so Litherland we have been beckoned to the bleakest moments,
dearest, & I wish I could wash you in them and them in you.
But I cannot, for all soft soap moments are a thing of the past.
Once upon a time we were tremendously civilised: Just look at the gleaming
washed & dried up dishes from the happy night before.
We rose one or the other to take our croissants from the
freezer. I went downstairs and wrote in jam: Don't leave me
in this highly unfortunate world upside down without you.

We kissed repeatedly. We kissed repeatedly and kissed again.
O darling Litherland, my love from middle England, now we are
in a war of raging bad misfortune and Shakespeare and Donne
are upon your shiny lips and I am not, Litherland. It is hopeless
and terrible utterly. This zestful union delegate now my beloved
but the harvest moone has waned and the horrible cycle refuses to be busted.
Thus my untumbled Soviet, strong and female to the utmost
all of my inherited pathetic Western sores and scarres & trials.
Our minor portion of spring's brilliant wake-up, our fiery delight
as the herb garden goes wild. Our one flower-fuming summer only.
And there are those around us who will talk and they will will say:
I laugh at your lemon balm, your chocolate mint, I am laughter
itself! Fleece she said nothing. Broken tongues and broken wings.
Broken swannes. No longer the lakeland laughter. Grim death comes.
And there would be those around us who would talk, and they
would say: not even half a year, it is nothing. They shattered
as the first frosts ironed out the very earth. They cracked as Jack
moved in like a saw and sawed the garden down. Autumn a stranger
to their love, winter beyond. I write alone with index finger dipped in deepest
snow: Please, love of my life, forever love of my life,
don't leave me in this harmful loveless world without you.
Not for them in ceaseless chatter the firelight & twinned & twined
limbs & toes. Boats. In a snowy world of imagined troikas &
tundras. Not for them the wonders of a huggable December. We
fell apart like charred and flaky Christmas wrapping paper.
I never meant to hurt you Shirley I can't go in the car it's impossible.
Even all of their whiteknuckle clinches dissolved in lakes of
alcohol I could never say goodbye to. Soviet sister, comrade,
tight as a freemason in my arms: I knew you would not, would not
relish the falling of the wall. If only together at the Finland Station.
But, darling, let's no longer smoothe no more. Let's go disgust.
And let me leave this strongly-written leaf from the destructed tree:
please dollypops don't leave me in this completely empty world without you.
Those cold fingers grasping winter grass. Frost seizing the heart.
All the fallow worldlings can hold their tongues now. All the fallow
wordlings can wait their late bus. My love welded into the air like

Lenin said as if I had a million hands with mighty sweep, as if if you were Lily
Brik, as if you were at the barricades, fighting the terrible
brokers of newspaper employees. And after a year you won!
That
          winter
                      your determined boots and feet.

Fawning into the wide-brimmed glasses of endless alcohol & gapingly
swallowing, you finally reach the darkest sideness. You put up with
the physical. Fight her lovely iris blue face in your red one. Ignore
her pouring tears filling every cup I know & say that's that, twat.

If only the rain would arrive finally and cool things down.
There is nothing left in the heather but death, death, death.
They have been here, they have killed the miners, they have
killed the swannemerchants. At dawn I scratch a plea upon
an appletree: don't leave me in this.

I wander, wonder, through the frozen roots, like JH Prynne, it is nothing,
it is nowt, I slay the slugs, I kiss the ends of the black earthe.
So near to the frozen treeline. Gunmen hiding there will have me
sooner than. Debris of misfortune & delay lies array around about us.

Lapus hearts we have destroyed, now that we have destroyed our
contract. Now that we have frozen the ghylls & utterly beautiful
becks & streams.

Don't despair don't leave me in this disunited universe without you.

No more the Durham train timetable, no more the loving departure
in Flass Vale or the twinning and twining of fast-moving limbs. Lambs
together cuddled in a huddle. In the shady shadow of the great viaduct
beneath the marigolds' sunlit vast spread, the luminous ones, bottercoppes.
Beneath the cowslips' shadows. And Pearl's a-a-a-a-a-a's.

No more steamed trainwindow wetrain fingertouching pale departures,
I am excused in the twilit world of hastily-summoned Paddy's Taxis,
I am in Paris, France, not Texas,
no more the palm-touching departure, steamed window of late trains.
No more the twilight world of midnight taxis, flinging me back
into the drunkenworld, from the tipsy rim of impossible places.
My staring starring contest with eyeless demons known only as
Knivesinne The Mouth and the rest of the block-booted mob
in the alcohol Stasi social work witch-hunt gang. Give me your babies!
I am here with the police and they have their sledgehammers!
It is 3 a.m! I am dressed in finest tweed and what will you do about

it, you stupid working class Kent scum? I'm a poet once & after all.
All the M20 and M2 Hell's Angel's are gone by the byre like my Bar
on his MotoGuzzi California. Frantic soup meets the mind, I lean into the
trees, blind. I have every opportunity to cancel the sunne! TO marry their
children. I revved there but I did not want it, only Paris, not even in the attic, I
did not, only seven, beaten to the floor
know Mayakovsky, Malevich, Shelley, Blake, Litherland, Notley.
I was alone with silent her in the fierce place of upland streams.
I was alone with her hazel brown eyes as the heavy rain sheeted down.
Then the Stalin KGB overcoats stamped on our wondrous faces &
turned their awesome mouthgaps upon us in the vivid tremor of a not-
drinking moment. O they stand against us like a really proper version,
like the perverted Christians who came in black to try and sort out your
tongue. They hurt you only and I wept alone in the sunlit marigold beds.

They have returned & are burning the shadows in movie
Expressionist fervour: all of those bats – pipistrelles – rustling
between their overcoated breastblades moving their huge coats
in terrifying unison. They have a demand in their hands. They
want me to be part of the torture along the blood-riven waveband.
They want me me to play a part in their play of the actually dead.
They now want my liver to explode in a shower of hot bloody starres.
They want me to die in vain, they want me to fax my useless expiration
to the head demon at the top of the stairs. O useless Jesus Christ
Almighty where now upon the hill is your broken working-class tree?
They came upon me in a herd of horror. Don't sting! Don't sting!
From the wet revs of the hospital car park over the road, from the
mumbles and grumbles of the released, flung into the West Road.
I return there, patient also, my hidden bottles, stuffed away corks.
They want me to come back they want me to come back they want me.
But in this terrible scary ghastly frightful world of endless nada
of the hearte please don't leave me in this lonely world without you.

1994-98

When The Lights Went Out A Cheer Rose in the Air

(for Steve Earle)

I had endless injections myself
and the drawing out of blood for tests

the endless withdrawing of blood for tests
the coming-to and then more tests

the crystal pipettes gleamed in the morning
and the tenderly professionally applied swab lint

I glanced through letter-box eyes at 6 o'clock
thinking the slightly waving drip an Armstrong strut

wind hammering through it or sweetly whistled
with a bed-end owl carved out of Canadian maple

yet the road sweeping from the end of the bed
was semi-coloned with frost-fringed dawheads

they – black as the brain of Ezra in St Elizabeth –
hung their beaks in the doll of my flung away dung

I shook like a broken Elswick rivet, a shattered
magnet in the coil of a brilliant engine, my very

Northern spirit. Maleable as a tarte au poivre
I leaned broken and speechless into the sister's hands

& I was alone in my single toll in my single iron bed
alone in my bed with the lungvictims hacking

I was alone at three in the morning, all the hymns
almost lost to history, the asbestosis lads on the

final run towards heaven and glory, down the
eternal slipways, down the vibration white finger funworld

from Swan Hunter to spirted out saliva kingdom.
I walk from bed to bed, a dawnmilk ghost myself,

fitted out, fitted in, fitting, unfitting, bruised busted
& broken, no more Billy Pigg pipes, I cannot remember

the heatherberry tunes in my skullshattered head:
Only ask the blackgrouse – he knows where I am

tonight – up a height alone in my trust bed, iron
rungs handy to loop my limbs, stop me from stalking

      stop me from talking, my broken tongue forking
      towards the argent moone, the sunne will betray me

      the oxygen exhaling & inhaling wards – 6, 7, 8, & 9,
      closing their prayer books and bibles, not the King

      James versions; I can, thanks to my eternal foresight,
      and my purchases over the years, read them poems

      from William Blake, not Billy Bloke, and Pursuit
      Shellac, that famous renegade England runaway:

      Withe his fast fury and strange politics, which burn
      like leadminefireseams, I love him like a wifely starre

and in the wet raindrop doglicking morning alone with the dying
as I was alone with them in the Bradford City football fire

I will not shut up I will not spend cash in the highly-recommended
to buy a beautifully-appointed needle with little hole in one end

to take the jade thread on a bobbin to pull it through and make
sure that it is even and perhaps tie a knot, I will not

Yes, it is true: I am a fantasticalist – like Mayakovsky I DO
want Victory Over The Sun! What's the point of living otherwise?

But alone in Ward 6 in my angel's shift I walk reading Billy Bloke
to the men with one lung and those with a poor stroke of bad luck

and wait alone with my books, a union man, a left wing man
with a right foot on the field of play, and shattered rivets

      the winding and rewringing
    of loved one's hands and the spewing

and taking of tablets to cease the nausea
and endless withdrawal detox puking
and ridiculous impossible breakfasts

and my fiery fierce love
in a swarm of desert snakes

I don't know how they live so dry
and me miserable to be soaked

trying with help to beat the shakes
the quakes the gulped-down lakes

still I wish innocent I was a childe
three days dead man walking dead men burning
released
signed out
first time only before all the next times
dead streets stalking   sober alone

hospital shadows mix with saliva on my energetic tongue.

They say I'll live again. Winter's dead. Spring sprung.

29 March – 19 May 1997

Sweet Advocate
(for Gillian Gibson)

Blizzard blossom's pink fumes: between
    low scrawling
the tender engine plans pursuit of bright ardency
    before swift return to facts.
O yet to seek is petals trembling, coursed
    with fire; a wrathless account.
Unhinged events divorced, as you will be
    from that money-sodden lout,
alone in his castle and counting mad cash.
    We will have justice
with bite, kisses on the Royal Mile perhaps,
    well-mannered in expressions
of faith. I am with you & beside myself
    in that mounted city
of joyous grandeur, that harps in our hearts
    and holds its breath.

We plan nothing because alarms come easy,
    ardency flagged-out.
From the toy museum to the wine bar
    it is a walk inside paradise.
Forgiveness seekers crawl with doubt.
    You can smell it in their faces.
Strapped for hard money & in a nutshell,
    creamed. What beckons
is a parliament of foes & sighs, yet

    the undamaged reverse
is also true. Your starched court cravat
    says so, blinding as the moon & sun.
Argent, blanche, and black are my favoured heart colours now.

Up then, away from procurator's shadow,
    along avenues for the briskest walk,
by strictest gardens where spires are dreamiest.
    How beautiful a city to have
such a beauty walking in its teeming mist & midst!
    Here, where I am today, behind this iron gate
where Newton's apple fell changing the world.
    Look, these are the rooms of JH Prynne.
Jesus Green is jazzed and fiery, beryl bicycles,
    lupins in a broth of flame.

Fainting at the smell of petals, cloud-heavy,
        looning at your click sharp shoes
& pronunciation brilliant so far from London.

        From single-toll to wide-awake:
so much good luck not to meet you
        in a witless time
with fuming ardour hanged in chains.

2
        Our world is very busy,
parterres aflame so much we have to seek
        a flower dictionary.
On & on & on & on & Up & down where changed,
        as we are like a tide,
and the whole themepark trembling. Let
        the scorning jay behave:
we have gathered so many convincing proofs,
        Shall we be forbidden
by manic thieves of cause & term? Blizzard
        blossom blazes by. Dew not gone,
yet the day is ours and all is brightest.
        Fancy that, most say,
passing by. Freed from winedrunk lethargy
        & passed-out lack of purpose,
the worker of good is truly beckoned on.

Your mind delicate as wing-tip kes feathers,
        without any false display.
To ruthless this would be fault by degree. Whole days
        of blockage chewing women
wildly-thorned. They were menace & a sin.
        Now it's us, laid down without
fancy decoration. The madhouse drinking
        closed. All taps turned off.

These fantastic bodyjolts quite famously
        relive their highland times:
the bedroom balletschool has opened again.
        To scran the testament
you say – adrift on pillows – Pierce me, yes,
        the pilgrim pleads,
but wait until 11 a.m. on Monday. Even so,

at the mammoth leaving desk, O you,
shoes are midnight charcoalblue, stepping
      out into a future not quite known.
Boozered by the bleat of stern children
      asking for more at midnight
never far away, the acolyte breathes uncertainty
      of pledged & promised dadhood.
Believe me, starched one, it's a damaged stream.

Remember how we walked across the greening lawn
      in Didsbury to talk to Win.
We stood in groups as jets descended
      & waved thumbs-up –
happy landings in the nation of nod.

    3

Total waste not in the scene; each blessed
      well looked-after garden
blooms & wakes up, This wild O'Hara world
      blinks too and shakes
its New York eyebrows at the sun. Each an island,
      it is said, and you leaned closer
when I said it, quoting Donne and Shelley,
      because the wind from the west
was booming the trunks in grey & blue.
      You said Rothko, or did you, person
brightest. Then the pen appeared & black ink
      thrived. What a poised italic nib.

We seize our breath, O this is a high place
      indeed, wings thronging
in a dream of freedom's flight away from
      all this ready muck.

Can you believe it is so real, say lips
      transferred into the permanence.
Frank & steady on the rock, marching
      to your arms from islands
of despair, where crashing waves are keenest.
      Quiet syllables beyond the hedge
drift here. Your left hand and costly golden ring.
      There is no closure of love
and all the tulips glow. The river
      of no return burns its banks
with heavy metal. No place for us there.

Help me somebody please
is a regular human message which does not
        blossom always into everyday song.
We try our lips and what we do in rainlight
        does not always become legend
except in the beating home of our hearts.

Another rush of jetted air trembles the
        good house. Hot displeasure
stroked my thighs. Gillian. I was a victim
        of true alienation, Othello-style.
O loveliness, yelps & moanings shook the ground.
        Pasturage not clean, jalousie
burned deep as fire, strange gods brooding.
        Even they were apprehensive.

4

It is true we go displumed, so much shopping
        to be done, in dampe of night
& terrorised. Your black suit against the wall.
        I am just a poet in love with you.

Beyond all of this and miles away the peewit cries
        lifting its green breast
from earth and earth's cares. It, like us,
        drags a wing for safety sure.
There is absolutely nothing false in that.

Yes, we are full-feathered, to taughten
        all for love, and love's
bright and brilliant mystery. Then we'll ride
        Shelley's mysterious light
and Shelley's weather forecast
        which blazes and shines
before the sinking of this deadened world.
        It is all stirred by breezes
my click heroine, and hold to say:
        All warnings have been received
from suspicious relatives, under what
        bright threshold & under
Newton's Cambridge tree. Then, treat-love,
        we may gather in absolute darkness
exchanging things far more fascinating than cash.

Savage in a trance he came.
That's what you'll say when I come back alone.
Wine-bar cronies
flogging their weeds in Edinburgh wind.
His madrage bids at lovemaking
made me unstable and crazy, not like an advocate at all.
I became by turns in my highland heart
mercurial and delicate. My eyelids – not to speak
of other places – unhinged & winged.

Then the anonymous letters dropped on the mat.
Forgive me, sweetheart I am an angry man
tonight. These overwhelming bits and things.
Possibilities are always passing clouds.
I seek you – and would love to call you darling –
from the broken pieces just as well.

May 1988 – April 1998
Northumberland–Edinburgh–Newcastle–Edinburgh

POSTCARDS FROM HITLER

[1998]

It's a collapsed empire

The Final Bavarian Hilltop Postcard

The bluebell sky, the sky of snowdrops.

Here, at the last count, where we we are,
daisies, dandelions and forget-me-nots.

At home, a late postcard from Adolf.

I cannot be there. No more Eva. No more Braun.
Too much happening. Six million.
I never counted having others do it.
Alien efficiency but the German sun
was never geared up and warm.

There was a needle and people less than me who disappeared swiftly.
I'll shave again in heaven and grieve my love:
The whole earth I never had.

30 March 1998

The Amazing Eagle Has Landed

Wank-fever ran the world before I came.
And the banks run by conspirators with long hooked noses.
You'll always call me an ex-corporal in the books of history.
It's always going to be a closed book to you, Jews
and Australians and publishers.
What the universe needed was charisma
and I provided it. Even George Orwell knew,
the least humorous man ever born on earthe.
I – me – single-handed and double-footed – put the words
National Socialist back into their rightful place.
We did not need poets or booksellers or badblood Jews.
I was particularly interested in the extermination of gypsies.
There was a purge on and I was all for it.
This was the outrageous age before nose-rings
and Gary Glitter but we enjoyed all of our behaviour.
Glory and tanks were the last two words we said before sleeping.

30 March 1998

Blitzkrieg Homage

Once I was a quiet man before Eva
Then the stars rose in the sky like enemies.
Assiduous in my beliefs – there was no room for poetry –
there were six zeroes separated halfway through only by a comma
and a six and a comma after that.
All of that in such a short time.
It was an amazing reign of terror and rage.
And a period of icy decision and we will be proud of it forever
as I was proud of it then.

Seeing St Paul's Cathedral
and the whole of Coventry burning made me come
very heavily
while Eva sucked my Nazi cock
and Goebels ranted
in due command
steadily,
saluting better than anyone.

31 March 1998

Let the Thunder Roll

I knew Stalin and knew him well.
Churchill even worse – not a new European.
Destroying you all was everything I craved.
Nobody left except the buttercups and milk of Germany.
In years to come, I imagined volk in pretty houses
installing old-fashioned Bakelite telephones
out of sheer nostalgia.
To me, it's an entirely putrid idea
because they don't match digital technology.

I don't want V2 rockets.
Fetch me nuclear power and fetch me Stalingrad.

31 March 1998

Whatever Madness There Is Is

Eva, my eternal spanked love, and Speer, before he went
the way of the rest of the Western world, cowardice
and betrayal scalded all over his pathetic back. V1s, V2s.

In my early days, I never touched a pfennig that hadn't
been handled by a Jew. It made me feel dirty and not German.

I spanked her because I liked it and she enjoyed it
especially the tougher it became. And I stared down
and ssnarled down Speer when his domination plan waved
in the wind.

Hands everything to me. Fists, palms, and pens for signing.
And the big open one high in the air.

31 March 1998

Brown stamps forever

We would sit alone in the Eagle's Nest
and spank and lie and speak about the business
of the future of the universe – one long poem unburdened
by myth and more black and white films than you care to name.

We never appreciated homosexuals and we never allowed in Negroes.
There was a repetitious revision of everything indeed.
Take your Satchmo and your Bessie back to where they came from.

There is a direness in my white sky. There is firmness in my purity.

And only I believe it.

31 March 1998

UNCOLLECTED POEMS

[1998–1999]

I Looked Down On a Child Today

I looked down on a child today, not because he or she was smaller than me
or because I was being in my middle-aged way bairnbarren and condescending
but because he or she was dying or dead between the kerbstone and the wheel

I stepped down from the steps of a 39 bus today with sudden blood on my shoes
The lesions and lessons and the languorous long-winged stiff-winged fulmars
chalked against the sky and white against the unpainted lips of her

I looked down at a child today, Gallowgate, the bus was turning left
the child stepped out, leaving its mam's hand behind partly swept by the wind
and partly by blind wonderful enthusiasm for life we guard against increasingly

She stepped into the path of something she or he would never know forever
in an elegant but unassuming place where as a living they hanged prisoners for
     bread-theft
it was the eve of St Valentine's Day on the wild side of Geordieland

The white dresses were being collected from dry cleaners Darn Crook to Sidgate
the strategy of the masses was being unaddressed once more except through the tills
where paper receipts come clicking out increasingly slowly to everyone's annoyance

What a beautiful, brilliant day, tart with expectation of love and romance in Chinatown
or down the Bigg Market as lager casks were moved into station and the dance
     floors cleaned
I looked down at a child today, never having had one of my own, and having no kid

I can call mine in a very old-fashioned romantic Barry MacSweeney Elvis Orbison
     Highway 61 way
O Robert it was almost where you left on the bus O Aaron O Dusty O Blackened
     Eyelids
I looked down upon a child today under the buswheels and knew whatever
     your name you would see

heaven and it would shine and be filled with pianos and trumpets and not be suppressed
and freedom would be written in moth-dust on every angel's wings
and there will be the music of Shostakovitch and Poulenc when you wanted to hear it

and the monumental poetry of MacDiarmid and Mahon and all spirits would
     gather there
and tell you when you awake again what lemonbalm was and you and say
I looked down on a child and bonnybairn in blood today the day before St
     Valentine's Day

Newcastle
13 February 1998

Totem Banking
(for JH Prynne)

The totemic fuse of non-events is rising like a fume
into a fakeless sky and then they are all disproved
by lapse into money greed and awesome self-possession
pathetic to the very bone fat and slavvering with wilful want
I seek them not but hold a flinty anger here on the high ground
no fat felines in this house we are lean and run like proper whippets

All sludge is there with bonus prize money cash right in hand
it sloughs upon the tide and happy too as the wallets scrap it up
wrestling with begotten tongues to say it's mine it's mine it's mine!
how short of true possession grandly ridden of their ever sense
amusing I suppose from those who have never heard of Bartok
but also how disgusting and pathetic and barbaric and eternally
backward standing there reeling at the latest arts council party

whingeing in a will of creepdom in their total victim stance
may they lie forever all together in their poverty and blame

the exact stance of the universe is completely improper
dark and shining in the night perhaps a file for copper
used by Shelley or Bunsen burner where are we again
alone upon the brow reiving at the downside fierce pierce

where are we arrow that flash of fletchering into the dawn
airport what airport vast expanse is it what do you mean expense
there is an animal at loose in my heart what kind of animal
poetry and a hatred of the tamed animals poets have become

we often lie upon the dark shore beaten by the different tide
but never crush the opposition flash it into the lights feel yourself
not least the black ptarmigan as it wings its brilliant skywards way
towards grass-free Tarmac out on the Nenthead road how sweet
for slag to be delivered by tractor instead of straight wheelbarrow
by you with your broken hair and broken throat don't mention it dear

Otherwise the wastrel pot is there but will never exceed us
for together we are lean and against all stupid wastage fantastick
it seems in the night how brill there are many people and many things
well that's fine sit down have a cuppa and a dry biscuit too
not to mention a dead leadmine way beyond the height of our brows

fizz fume the distant dance the electric trance
the nowhere brood strangled connections failed
correspondents largesse merchants house of Mammon
how hard the ground to stalk across wrapped with wimps
moaners fruitless no ones yet still the Tarmac is gorgeous

crapping for a laugh in a country so diseased by pride & failure
under the allotments of heaven which nobody has noticed lately
for want of attention Punch and Judys all happy by the seaside
of their tideless lives what is that other word for jetteurs? Ah yes to
remember every avenue from the dim lights of Sacre Coeur
to Rue St Denis 1000 steps Laforgue nitrates washed down the pipes

ghastly importance peacocked around by strutting dwarfs
their time-frozen feathers lathered with crass shadows darkness
even they want so much without heading for it life on a raft
of brisking around the meniscus on a wing and a cheque book
rain so insistent flashing in worse than the collected works
of illegitimates everywhere as they treacle their supposedly upward

o scorched stars of yesterday homaging fromaging other failures
thank you Margaret who started this ill fire furred starred with greed
without moral combustion slack distasteful wallets extraordinaire
here we are then upon the gunmetal road without Pearl perle
rain sheeting down running now a river along the curve in the path

as we head for frontiers a handful almost not the ignorant or studied
by far between the blessed planets dearest you are there also
inventing many wondrous things and nothing nothing less than zero
can remove that from us not to name the names but we are there
applied to the advancement of history and all hoorays to that
and damn the rest to the banking system all false totems burned

April 1999

Here We Go

And all we could hear was the smelt of bottercoppes
raging in the morning air desperate for attention.
In the English mini-universe so many poetic fops
brick their baseness. Unavoidable powderpuffs mention

all and everything. The blankness is amazing. Grind
into the unblessed machine which is zero, phewed
to the volcano of nothingness. Sedgeless & despined
we flee the beautiful night towards the dawn, crewed

and ready: pulpit swabbed, sonar pouting in the foredeck
green as grass from every dog-filled park. Dry Salvages
pass in dreaded mist, by some. I am buttoned, drecked
of everything, tranced to matters, scorning savages

looning the horizon and the sky. Masters' boys
and girls will fawn and fetch, like electroplated toys.

2 June 1999

PEARL IN THE SILVER MORNING

(1999)

Cushy Number

Much desired landscape loved keenly several lifetimes
Our unregenerated soil-heap hillsides, bleak
and bare of plastic life: one everyday religion.

Your ghost spindrifts in the lead-crusted law,
in mist combed by bracken and fern. The old school
where you were humiliated and betrayed, thrown

back to the riverbank and cribs of marigold, head
shaved, now up for sale: bijou conversion possibilities
for the turbo-mob, weird souls dreaming of car-reg

numbers and mobile phone codes. They are taking
over from the Barbour vegetarians, who couldn't
stand the nailed-down winters. Inside you, spectre,

an inarticulate fury. Me, tongue-boy, lathered with words,
and you, thee, fern-haired and Pearl naked. We swam
against all Tyne tides which rose from the sea. When you sink

towards the head of the hush, where the beck runs
out of the tunnel towards the west, brewing foam
as it goes, we'll meet my adverbs ad infinitum:
tongue-stoned invisible prelate of the shaking holes.

Bare Feet In Marigolds

First always the birds, buds, the wind-driven wild
running burn. Each morning, each season, so high in the sky.
Before it turned into a barbed wire compound.

Wild freedom of Sparty Lea turned into a Nazi camp.
Pride brought it down to this, wild self-willed pride,
family difference, sister and brother, and wild unlifting

everlasting vanity. Pull down I say pull down, but it
was too late. We stand together upon the peak and crest
your tongue still clucking and purring. You're the real poet!
You point at
                the clouds sweeping from Ireland towards the forgotten

sad hotels of Dunbar. Chucklehen, hazel-haired and eyed,
you always were the best. The two daughters you have now
in Haltwhistle and a strong husband who works from dawn
till end of day. Strong and upright and heavenly Tom strong.

I've lost my new love. Nowt, blown away

                            feathery leaf, upland wind.

Daft Patter

If anyone knows about sullen loneliness, you do
Yet there's a grin in the wind, heartless and cold
There's dark in the darkness, beauty of streams
I low my beams to you, from tunnel to tunnel

as if the frozen air had a distinct personality
Standing at the lonnen head, holding leeks, you
sawed my glance in half with yours. What keen eyes!
Such strange, out-dated clothes. What's inside counts.

Leaning into the tall grass grandness of your alert stance
towards the west and the brilliant beauties of Ireland,
I know now why you took the sickle hook
backing the beasts into their shutdown shed

You chopped the gate for want of sound
but you had sound, all sound, my purr mistress
my fantastic slavver merchant, when we peeled the sky

together we had water and silence and fire and togetherness
the lights of all you didn't say knots my life and all dreams.

Pearl In The Silver Morning

Slit of light across the sky above the city: 7 a.m:
raining and me wandering
Pearl in her moonshawl
in the sky gazing down at me – saying,
stay cool just like the frost on the lawns.
You'll melt in time.
Your broken heart will be warmed again.
Just look at the upcoming sunne.
Anger is hot, and Bar you have too much of it.

Passion is fine, fine, a fine gripping thing,
like we gripped fingers
by the Prudhoe bluebell beds, but hot temper is not.
We were hot, but never blasted
                            were we
                  like the clearing at night of the Consett Steelworks
ovens before the Pharisees shut them down.

Do you remember the flames we saw
from the rim of the law
holding hands   and although *you* spoke
it was *my* tongue and cleft palate
                            also containing music, music, music,
and we breathed
in each other's mouths, so young – innocent even – and the flames high
200 feet from the ovens in the air
                  like Blake's vision of Adam in the arms of heaven
of which you told me.

God help us
you full of talk of a city called Edinburgh
and me in silence so very deep we were so very much in love.

And the burns and sikes and streams
though shallow
were deep music to us.
You trout-tickler,
                  you flower-picker,
                            climber in willow trees, me laughing below

as best I could laugh, though you never thought it ugly.
Indeed the word you used was the word beautiful,
pinning cowslips behind my ears,

you patting and running fingers through our
beckwashed hair.
Lying by the marigold beds
bare toes entwined, then dancing under branches
before the elms ever died. But our mutual hearts never did.

Bar it is 7 and your raining rage
must cease
under my morning moon.
In my dawn shawl looking dawndown upon you
in your foot-striding fellhighhighupuptopheavyrainbeatingrainrain.
We have always walked together so long.
In the long grass we walked and walked forever so long so very language long
and I could say so once you had the slate in my lap.

My tongue blank – FOREVER, word we wrote on a slate, remember
when you taught me? – only my hands and eyes moving now – two
daughters we could have had –

but I am looking kindly and lovingly on you
Please do it
          – cool your raging fire lovelorn heart – for me.

And love me – forever.

We Are Not Stones

Darkly-harnessed light will fall like a shawl
and be the hunky-dory
death of us all. A hawk-wing death,
a shrike strike death, a death in a lair.
This mossy path, frilled with feldspar
to prick your pearly toes, fresh from the marigolds,
the little stile not squeaking now, lubricated
hinges, hymns to the silence of adult interference,
new sunken screwheads glinty in sunlight,
the death of the white linen: our cot-death.
It was all, all of it, all for us, from the wonders
of our mysterious heaven
to the trout's opal seed-sac bubbling with jewels.
The water was anointment water,
a cool upland baptism. You, you
were Delilah and Mary-of-the-tears,
of the unspoiled lips lapping rushing whitewater.
Milton was a blind man and we knew nothing of him.
Paradise Lost to the ears of his daughter.
Where are they now, our camps of wild primrose?
Now we are adults too, all grown-up.
You're there, I'm here, miles from our happiness.
We are not stone, but we are in the grinder.
Everything is lost, and we are dust and done for.

INDEX OF TITLES & FIRST LINES

(Titles are shown in italics, first lines in roman type.)

After copulation, 62
All aboard, it's party time, with, 206
All of you with consonants and vowels, 211
alone on Ranter's Rock, 159
And all we could hear was the smelt of bottercoppes, 317
'and the warm weather is holding', 42
& tie strings together, 41
Angel Showing Lead Shot Damage, 230
Anne Sexton Blues, 263
Argent moon with bruised shawl, 197
Arrest me asleep, crashed out, 238

Banged my right hand, 202
Bare Feet In Marigolds, 321
BBC monochrome newsreel flickers, 74
Beak Ode, 55
beaming Anaconda of parthian monumentalism your, 45
bee-like, 68
Beneath the worm's eye view people. The clubfoot, 132
Beulah, 39
Blackbird, 82
Black Torch Sunrise, 74
Blitzkrieg Homage, 311
Blizzard blossom's pink fumes: between, 304
Blizzard: So Much Bad Fortune, 212
Blossom Ode:Eltham Palace, 66
Brother Wolf, 23
Brown stamps forever, 312
Buying Christmas Wrapping Paper on January 12, 222

Cavalry At Calvary, 206
Chatterton Ode ('sleek beasts...'), 40
Chatterton Ode ('Time is a jagged mark...'), 37
Chaucer came here, 66
Colonel B, 88
Comb the crawling morning chill chilling sky in search for vodkafire, 255
Crepuscular phantoms energise manhood, soap, 48
Cry and she wanders, through, 50
Cushy Number, 320

Daddy Wants to Murder Me, 225
Daft Patter, 322
Darkly-harnessed light will fall like a shawl, 325
Dark Was the Night and Cold Was the Ground, 208
Dead Man's Handle, 255
death beholder, 46

329

Demons, big-hatted and hard-hatted, far as gutter-toppled, 237
Demons in My Pocket, 238
Demons Swarm upon Our Man and Tell the World He's Lost, 244
Disease Ode Carrot Hair, 51
Don't Leave Me, 295
Down from the rain-soaked law, 198
Dream Graffiti, 67
Dunce Ode, 47

Eva, my eternal spanked love, and Speer, before he went, 312

Far Cliff Babylon, 78
Fever, 203
Finnbar's Lament, 179
First always the birds, buds, the wind-driven wild, 321
Flamebearer, 170
Flame Ode ('and the warm weather is holding...'), 42
Flame Ode ('Make your naked phone call moan...'), 57
Flame Ode ('Two hawks and a plover swoop...'), 36
For Andrei Voznesensky, for her, 12
Forgive me for my almost unforgivable delay, 218
Fox Brain Apple Ode, 52
Free Pet with Every Cage, 220
From The Land Of Tumblestones, 207
Fusillade of the sun's eye-piercing darts, 216

Get out the shotgun put it in the gunrack, 220
Gnashed fervour licks down like fire, 233
God bless you little girl the lean dry hand, 189
God forgive me, 179
Good morning Pearl, good morning John, 204
Grassblade glintstreak in one of the last mornings, 199

Hammers and pinions, sockets, fatal faces, 209
Hellhound Memos, 185-92
her name was Bonney and although she wasn't registered, 44
Her wild oregano, 61
Here We Go, 317
Himself Bright Starre Northern Within, 257
Homage to John Everett, Marine Painter, 1876-1949, 33
Hooray Demons Salute the Forever Lost Parliament,
How sweet today the scents and air perfumes, 249

I am gnawing jawface, furman, odd cove, 253
I am irregular as poker chips, 12
I could never speak, 210
If anyone knows about sullen loneliness, you do, 322
I had endless injections myself, 301
I knew Stalin and knew him well, 311

I'll be down at the dock in the morning, 191
I Looked Down On a Child Today, 314
In with the Stasi, 233
Indigo robe her arm is wrapped within. Amber, 37
Influx of new crass mourning. Shrouds, 38
I put my walking stick, 53
Irish poets, 292
I smashed my wings, 195
I tear apart the smart brochures, 212
i walk to the annexe, 33
I write poetry at the age of seven and daddy wants to murder me, 225

Jim Morrison Ode, 37
John Bunyan to Johnny Rotten, 284
Jury Vet, 101
Just Twenty Two – And I Don't Mind Dying, 20

Kein Eingang Liz gone hard from the broken phallic window, 95

La Rage, 292
Lash Ode, 53
Last night tells me today what went, 15
Let loose at morning from frost pockets the wind rips, 222
Let the Thunder Roll, 311
Let's dab a double finger half-pissed kiss on Muddy's lips. O, 230
Levellers and prince-fingerers quartered in the heather, 190
Linda Manning Is a Whore, 190
Listen, hark, attend; wait a moment, 196
Liz Hard, 95
Liz Hard II, 99
Looking Down From The West Window, 195
Lost Pearl, 213

Make your naked pencil mine. Play, 58
Make your naked phone call moan, listen, 57
Me the multiplex moron, multigenerational, 187
Mia Farrow, 61
Mony Ryal Ray, 200
Moon afloat, drunken opal shuggy boat, 215
Moon Ode, 39
Much desired landscape loved keenly several lifetimes, 320
My hands are in the clouds again, thumping the sun, 213

NAZI neon burned the blitzkrieg heart Liz hid, 99
New Ode, 37
Nil by Mouth: The Tongue Poem, 237
No Buses To Damascus, 201
No Such Thing, 199
Nothing Are These Times, 253

Now it's time to put aside and forget, 246
Now that the vast furtherance of widespread publicity, 188

Ode, 43
Ode Black Spur, 60
Ode Grey Rose, 46
Ode Long Kesh, 41
Ode Peace Fog, 50
Ode:Resolution, 56
Odes, 35-72
Ode Stem Hair, 48
Ode to Beauty Strength and Joy and in Memory of the Demons, 218
Ode to the Unborn, 44
Ode White Sail, 59
of Barry and Jacqueline, 246
O hello, Othello, black and green bastardo, 266
O just to vex me inside the bottle the wind stayed still, 275
OKAY CRIMSON VARNISHED REDHEAD YOU'RE THE BIG
    ATTRACTION NOW, 101
O let me plunge my feverhands into his clotted throat. Let me free, 224
Once I was a quiet man before Eva, 311
On the Burning Down of the Salvation Army Men's Palace, Dogs Bank,
    Newcastle, 14
O pulchritudinous orb de la dish scourer, 49
O pusilanimous orb de la Brillo, 47
O the rare gold, 207
Open your black-backed gull, 55
Orphan consorts & vipers under glass. Hair, 88

Panther Freckles, 49
Pasolini Demon Memo, 235
Pass the aconite, 56
Pearl, 193-216
Pearl Against the Barbed Wire, 249
Pearl Alone, 205
Pearl and Barry Pick Rosehips for The Good of the Country, 209
Pearl at 4 a.m., 215
Pearl: beautiful lustre, highly prized gem, 208
Pearl, I'm singing Fever to you, 203
Pearl In The Silver Morning (poem), 323
Pearl in the Silver Morning (sequence), 319-25
Pearl Says, 198
Pearl Suddenly Awake, 202
Pearl's Final Say-So, 216
Pearl's Poem of Joy and Treasure, 214
Pearl's Utter Brilliance, 197
Peristalsis writhes a sudden knot &, 38

Phantom, phantom, 163
Postcards from Hitler, 309-12

Rain, rain, rain again and bonerolling bloodthunder, 248
Ranter (poem), 140
Ranter (sequence), 139-177
Ranter loping, 140
Ranter's Reel, 163
Real Ode, 63
Rock litmus. Titration from Springfield, she, 20
rude unwelcome guest, 82

Sample the hardness, trite mania, 51
Selected from the gutter realm, 67
Shaking Minds with Robespierre, 190
She walks up. Stands in the air. It is raining, 39
Show me the door, 59
Shreds of Mercy/ The Merest Shame, 231
Shunned, ignored, cast off, slung in the bin, 231
Skybrightness drove me, 200
sleek beasts, 40
Slit of light across the sky above the city: 7 a.m, 323
Smartism seems to be the best deal, 244
Snake Paint Sky, 45
Snipe Drumming, 159
So there you are lying down here breasts, 265
Spangled balconies abound, 52
Spout, pout, spout. Put my spittle all about, 214
Spurs of neonised leather, 60
Strap Down in Snowville, 266
Sunk at my crossroads, hellhounds baying, 186
Sunk in my darkness at daylight, 186
Swedenborg Ode, 38
Sweeno is two people – at least. Sweeno the night crawling homme man, 269
Sweeno, Sweeno, 269
Sweet Advocate, 304
Sweet Jesus: Pearl's Prayer, 196

The Amazing Eagle Has Landed, 310
The bluebell sky, the sky of snowdrops, 310
The Book of Demons, 217-90
The feet are white boats. Hands are, 36
The Final Bavarian Hilltop Postcard, 310
the fire-crowned terrain, 23
The Horror, 242
The horror of the hospital for us both, 242
The Jesus Christ Almighty is a barely stripling bare-chested biker, 235
The Last Bud, 15

The long shadows of gold October stamped into the earth of England, 284
There is absolutely no record, 257
The Shells Her Auburn Hair Did Show, 204
The totemic fuse of non-events is rising like a fume, 315
The very low odour tough acrylic formula, 188
They stood smoking damp and salvaged, 14
This is the dirt, far, 54
Those Sandmartin Tails, 210
Time is a jagged mark upon the wrist. See, 37
Tom in the Market Square Outside Boots, 280
Tom you're walking up & down the pill hill again, 280
Torchlit smoulderer, 170
Torpedo, 58
Totem Banking, 315
Trouble on all side today up and down, 189
Two hawks and a plover swoop, 36

Underneath the western starres, my heart is sore, 295
Up a Height and Raining, 275
Urals postmaster, this is your, 43

Vapour rises from the ducts and flues, ashen and feathered, 192
Viper Suck Ode, 62
Vixen Head / What Small Hands, 54

Wank-fever ran the world before I came, 310
We Are Not Stones, 325
Wedding rings & tears. You are on, 63
We Offer You One Third Off Plenitude, 224
We would sit alone in the Eagle's Nest, 312
Whatever Madness There Is Is, 312
what would life be without Johann Boetticher, 39
When the Candles Were Lit, 248
When The Lights Went Out A Cheer Rose in the Air, 301
Wild Knitting, 132
Wing Ode, 36
Wisdom flew upon me tonight like a bat's wing, 190
Woe, Woe, Woe, 211
Woke up this morning, 263
Wolf Tongue, 68
Wonder Pearl distemper pale, queen, 201
Wringing the Shingle, 191

Yes, I am not emitting articulate sound, 205
Your Love Is a Swarm and an Unbeguiled Swanne, 265

Reading Barry MacSweeney

edited by PAUL BATCHELOR

Barry MacSweeney was described as 'a contrary, lone wolf... [whose] ear for a soaring lyric melody was unmatched' (Nicholas Johnson, *Independent*). MacSweeney found fame with his first book, *The Boy from the Green Cabaret Tells of His Mother*, which appeared when he was just nineteen years old. But he soon retreated from the publicity, and for almost thirty years his poetry appeared only in small press publications. Identifying himself with Chatterton and Rimbaud, MacSweeney developed a poetics based on experiment and excess, from the fragmented lyricism of 'Brother Wolf' to the political anger of 'Jury Vet'; from the dizzying historical perspectives of *Ranter* to the nightmarish urban landscape of *Hellhound Memos*.

In 1997, MacSweeney once again found a wider audience, with the publication of his last full-length book, *The Book of Demons*, which recorded his fierce fight against alcoholism. This book also included *Pearl*, a sequence of tender lyrics celebrating the poet's first love and his rural Northumbrian childhood. At the time of his death in 2000, MacSweeney was preparing a retrospective selection of his work for publication. When *Wolf Tongue: Selected Poems 1965-2000* appeared in 2003, it brought a wealth of poetry back into print, displaying the incredible range, ambition and quality of MacSweeney's work.

Reading Barry MacSweeney is the first book of essays to assess MacSweeney's achievement. Bringing together academic critics, poets and friends of the poet, the book considers many aspects of MacSweeney's career, including his political verse, his re-imagining of pastoral poetry, his love of popular music, and his mapping of Northumberland. Contributors include Professor W.N. Herbert, Matthew Jarvis, Peter Riley, Professor William Rowe, Harriet Tarlo and Professor John Wilkinson, as well as MacSweeney's journalist friend Terry Kelly, and poet S.J. Litherland, MacSweeney's former partner.

Paperback   ISBN 978 1 85224 988 5   208 pages

Milton Keynes UK
Ingram Content Group UK Ltd.
UKHW021955090624
443913UK00008B/340